THE SCHWEICH LECTURES ON
BIBLICAL ARCHAEOLOGY, 1930

ANCIENT SYNAGOGUES
IN PALESTINE
AND GREECE

OXFORD UNIVERSITY PRESS
AMEN HOUSE, E.C. 4
LONDON EDINBURGH GLASGOW
LEIPZIG NEW YORK TORONTO
MELBOURNE CAPETOWN BOMBAY
CALCUTTA MADRAS SHANGHAI
HUMPHREY MILFORD
PUBLISHER TO THE
UNIVERSITY

KAFR BIR'IM, PORTAL OF MAIN SYNAGOGUE

ANCIENT SYNAGOGUES
IN PALESTINE
AND GREECE

BY

E. L. SUKENIK

ARCHAEOLOGIST TO THE INSTITUTE OF JEWISH STUDIES OF THE
HEBREW UNIVERSITY, JERUSALEM

THE SCHWEICH LECTURES

OF THE BRITISH ACADEMY

1930

LONDON

PUBLISHED FOR THE BRITISH ACADEMY

BY HUMPHREY MILFORD, OXFORD UNIVERSITY PRESS

AMEN HOUSE, E.C.

1934

PRINTED IN GREAT BRITAIN
AT THE UNIVERSITY PRESS, OXFORD
BY JOHN JOHNSON
PRINTER TO THE UNIVERSITY

IN MEMORY OF

Sɪʀ ISRAEL GOLLANCZ

זכרונו לברכה

PREFACE

THE present volume agrees in substance but not in form with the lectures which I delivered, upon the invitation of the British Academy, in the autumn of the year 1930; and indeed it can hardly be otherwise when lantern-slide lectures are reduced to book form with a limited number of illustrations. For here, on the one hand, greater discoursiveness must largely take the place of ocular demonstration, and on the other a reference which the reader may look up at his leisure can often suffice where some explanation is indispensable to an audience of listeners. In thus adapting myself to the exigencies of the written medium, I have also been led to modify the original arrangement of the material. I feel that in making these departures I have only served the best interests of those for whom these chapters are destined.

In giving the final English form to these lectures, I was greatly assisted by Dr. H. L. Ginsberg, Jerusalem, to whom I am also indebted for many valuable suggestions.

The bulk of the photographs reproduced here belong to the collection of the Archaeological Department of the Hebrew University, Jerusalem. For the photographs and drawings from the synagogue of Na'aran I am much obliged to the Dominican Fathers, RR. PP. L. H. Vincent and R. Savignac. For the photographs of the portal of the now non-existent synagogue ruin of Kafr Bir'im (Pl. XVI), the plan of the Synagogue at Jerash (Fig. 9), and for the figure of the Ark at Peqi'in (Fig. 13), I am indebted to the Palestine Exploration Fund; for the plan of Delos to Prof. Pierre Roussel, Director of the École Française d'Athènes; for the drawing of the mosaic pavement at the synagogue of Aegina to Dr. G. Welter; to my colleagues Prof. L. A. Mayer for help in reading the manuscript and proofs, and Dr. M. Schwabe for valuable suggestions when we discussed Judaeo-Greek inscriptions; to Prof. W. F. Albright for reading a proof and Miss Th. Goell for help in compiling the index.

This volume is dedicated to the memory of the late Sir Israel Gollancz, upon whose initiative I was invited to deliver these lectures. It was a great shock to me, as to all his friends, to learn of his untimely death, which took place some time before the lectures were given.

I take this opportunity to reiterate my thanks to the Printer and the readers of the Oxford University Press for their interest and care in producing this volume.

CONTENTS

PAGE

PREFACE vii

LIST OF PLATES xi

LIST OF FIGURES IN THE TEXT xiii

LIST OF ABBREVIATIONS xv

CHAPTER I
Origin and Significance of the Synagogue.—Explora-
tion of Synagogues.—The Synagogue at Capernaum.—
The Synagogue at Chorazin.—The Synagogue at Kafr
Bir'im I

CHAPTER II
Development of Synagogue Architecture.—Na'aran.—
Beth Alpha.—Jerash.—Synagogues in Greek Lands.—
Delos.—Miletus.—Priene.—Aegina . . . 27

CHAPTER III
Architecture of Synagogues.—Situation of Synagogues.
—Orientation of Synagogues.—Interior Equipment of
Synagogues.—Ornamentation of Synagogues.—Dating
of Synagogues.—Inscriptions 46

APPENDIX
The Synagogue of Stobi.—Ḥammath-by-Gadara.—
Dura Europos.—The Synagogue at 'Esfia on Mount
Carmel 79

INDEX 87

LIST OF PLATES

Frontispiece   Kafr Bir'im, portal of main synagogue.

PLATE

I *a* Capernaum, north-west corner of synagogue, restored.
  b Capernaum, northern colonnade of synagogue, restored.
II *a* Capernaum, lintel of main doorway.
  b Capernaum, lintel of main gate to the courtyard.
  c Capernaum, lintel of the second gate to the courtyard.
III *a* Capernaum, keystone of arched window.
  b Capernaum, frieze on the façade, defaced figures of lion.
IV *a* Capernaum, benches on the west side.
  b Capernaum, frieze.
V *a* Capernaum, frieze.
  b Capernaum, frieze.
  c Capernaum, carruca.
VI Capernaum, stones of frieze resting on pilaster capitals.
VII *a* Capernaum, courtyard, corner capital.
b, c Capernaum, courtyard, capital.
VIII *a* Chorazin, general view looking south.
  b Chorazin, general view looking north-east.
IX Jerash, synagogue, mosaic floor.
X Delos, general view of synagogue.
XI Aegina, mosaic floor of synagogue.
XII *a* Ḥammath-by-Tiberias, stone candlestick.
  b Ḥammath-by-Tiberias, screen.
XIII *a, b* Capernaum, fragments of lion.
  c Kafr Bir'im, head of lion.
XIV Ascalon, screen.
XV Chorazin, seat of Moses.
XVI *a* Jerusalem, Ophel, inscription of Theodotos.
  b Kafr Bir'im, doorway with inscribed lintel of small synagogue (now non-existent).
XVII *a* Capernaum, Greek inscription.
  b Capernaum, Aramaic inscription.
XVIII *a, b* Na'aran, Mosaic inscriptions.
XIX Map of Palestine, showing sites with synagogue.

LIST OF FIGURES IN THE TEXT

FIG. 1 Capernaum, plan of synagogue.

FIG. 2 Chorazin, sketch-plan of synagogue.

FIG. 3 Kafr Bir'im, restoration of synagogue after Kohl and Watzinger.

FIG. 4 Na'aran, plan of synagogue.

FIG. 5 Na'aran, mosaic floor, Zodiac.

FIG. 6 Na'aran, mosaic floor. Ark with two candlesticks.

FIG. 7 Beth Alpha, plan of synagogue.

FIG. 8 Beth Alpha, diagram of main mosaic floor.

FIG. 9 Jerash, plan of synagogue and later church.

FIG. 10 Delos, stadion and synagogue.

FIG. 11 Miletus, plan of synagogue.

FIG. 12 Priene, plan of synagogue.

FIG. 13 Peqi'in, figure of ark.

FIG. 14 Jewish gilt glass.

FIG. 15 Lamp with figures of synagogual appurtenances.

FIG. 16 Jewish gilt glass.

FIG. 17 Aleppo Bema.

FIG. 18 Ḥammath-by-Tiberias, seat of Moses.

FIG. 19 Delos, seat of Moses.

LIST OF ABBREVIATIONS

b.   = Babylonian Talmud.

CAIL   = *Comptes Rendus de l'Académie des Inscriptions et Belles-Lettres.*

j.   = Jerusalem (Palestinian) Talmud.

JPOS   = *Journal of the Palestine Oriental Society.*

PEF. Q. St. = *Palestine Exploration Fund, Quarterly Statement.*

RB   = *Revue Biblique.*

REJ   = *Revue des Études Juives.*

ZAW   = *Zeitschrift für die alttestamentliche Wissenschaft.*

ZNW   = *Zeitschrift für die neutestamentliche Wissenschaft.*

CHAPTER I

1. *Origin and Significance of the Synagogue.*

THE problem of the origin of the Synagogue is, properly speaking, outside the purview of these lectures; which are primarily concerned with the physical features of the Jewish houses of worship at a time when the institution of the Synagogue had already crystallized. A brief summary of the very conflicting views that are held on this subject will, however, no doubt be of interest. Some scholars go so far as to claim a pre-Exilic origin for the Synagogue. They believe that houses of prayer and study existed in Palestine side by side with the First Temple and its sacrificial ritual. Others, more plausibly, date the origin of the Synagogue in the period of the Babylonian Exile at the very earliest. They argue that it was the Exile that caused the Temple to lose some of its original unique significance and favoured the appearance of local houses of worship.[1]

It is also a matter of dispute whether the first synagogues are to be sought in Palestine or in the lands of the ancient Diaspora. It may be interesting to note in this connexion that whereas there is archaeological evidence of the existence of synagogues in Egypt as early as the third century B.C.E.,[2] and in Greece as early as the second century B.C.E.,[3] the date of the oldest remains of a synagogue found in Palestine is not earlier than the first century C.E.[4]

---

[1] See S. Krauss, *Synagogale Altertümer*, Berlin-Vienna, 1922, pp. 52 ff., for an account of the various views put forward; among most recent writers on the question may be mentioned L. Finkelstein, 'The Origin of the Synagogue', *Proc. Amer. Acad. for Jewish Research*, New York, 1928–30, pp. 49 ff., and A. Menes, 'Tempel und Synagoge', *ZAW*, 1932, pp. 268 ff.

[2] Namely, a synagogue inscription from the ancient Schedia quarter of Alexandria, dated in the reign of Ptolemy III, Euergetes (247–221 B.C.E.); *v.* T. Reinach, 'Sur la date de la colonie juive d'Alexandrie', *REJ*, 1902 (xlv), pp. 161 ff.; *v.* also E. Schürer, *Geschichte des jüdischen Volkes*, 4. Aufl., iii, p. 41.   [3] *v.* p. 40.   [4] *v.* p. 69.

Whatever the time and circumstances under which the Synagogue originated, however, there can be no doubt concerning its significance as a new departure in the history of religion. Renan rightly names it 'la création la plus originale et la plus féconde du peuple juif'. It is difficult for us to realize how revolutionary to the ancient world was a form of worship that excluded alike initiation by mysteries and propitiation by offerings. From the Synagogue it was taken over by Christianity, and later by Islam.[1]

2. *Exploration of Synagogues.*

Turning now to the study of actual remains of ancient synagogues in Palestine, we must begin by mentioning the Jewish pilgrims of the Middle Ages who came from the lands of the Diaspora to Palestine in order to prostrate themselves at the tombs of the Prophets, Scholars, and Saints. At this time the Jews had already abandoned many of the places where ancient remains are to be found. It is, however, remarkable, and in a way rather touching, to note how the people cherished the associations of these spots, and how, almost suddenly, a swarm of traditions seemed to spring up about them, making them the burial-grounds of kings and saints—as though with the desire of ensuring them against oblivion. The littérateurs among the pilgrims who came to pray at these supposed tombs described them in their texts, and it is here that we encounter the earliest, if only incidental, references to the remains of old synagogues. In fact, by comparing the accounts of different authors we can follow the progressive decay of these venerable monuments in the course of the centuries. This disintegration is of course partly due to the destructive work of fanatics or to the hand of time, but also to some extent to the depredations of the ignorant people of the neighbourhood, who applied the stones of these, as of other, ruins to various utilitarian purposes. It is worth noting that the pilgrims

[1] Cf. G. F. Moore, *Judaism in the First Centuries of the Christian Era*, Cambridge, Mass., i, pp. 281 ff.

remarked the peculiar features of the synagogues, and assumed them to be the work of Rabbi Simeon ben Yoḥai, a scholar of the second century c.e., a date which approximately coincides with the results of modern archaeological research.[1]

Since the beginning, early last century, of the scientific exploration of Palestine and its antiquities, our knowledge of these remains has become more exact. The first scholar to describe them in greater detail, the Rev. Edward Robinson, was on his first journey in 1838 as yet unable to determine their character.[2] During his second sojourn in 1852, however, he identified them as ruins of ancient synagogues.[3] In the interval between these two visits, the ruins had been explored by several other scholars and travellers, who had already inferred their true character by means of the Hebrew inscriptions found on some of them

[1] Curiously, the earliest of the medieval Jewish travellers, Benjamin of Tudela, an observant man who visited Palestine in the years between 1160 and 1173, makes no mention of ancient synagogues. The first notice of them is contained in the itinerary of R. Samuel b.-R. Samson, who made a pilgrimage to the Holy Land in the year 1210 c.e. This work was published for the first time by E. Carmoli, who translated it into French from a manuscript in the Ducal Library of Parma, as part of a collection entitled *Itinéraires de la Terre Sainte*, Brussels, 1847. This was followed by an edition of the original Hebrew text of the same manuscript in *Ozar Tob* (אוצר טוב) by A. Berliner and D. Hoffmann (Hebrew supplement to the *Magazin für die Wissenschaft des Judentums*), Berlin, 1878. Unfortunately, the copyist of this MS. did not preserve the whole of R. Samuel's account, but only extracted from it the portion describing the author's journey from Jerusalem to Nineveh; and besides parts of the text seem to have got displaced, thus sometimes misleading scholars into erroneous conclusions. A critical edition of this and other Jewish Palestine itineraries is a desideratum.

On this itinerary see also Sukenik in *Ṣiyyon* (Journal of the Palestine Historical and Ethnographical Society, in Hebrew), ii, pp. 108 ff.

[2] E. Robinson, *Biblical Researches in Palestine and in Adjacent Regions*, second edition, Boston, 1860, ii, pp. 406 ff.

[3] E. Robinson, *Later Biblical Researches*, &c., second edition, Boston, 1857, pp. 70, 74, 342, 346.

and the information they were able to gather from the Jews of Galilee and the Arabs living round about. The discovery of the Sarcophagus of Eshmunazar in Sidon inspired the French Government to send out a scientific expedition to Phoenicia, headed by Ernest Renan. In 1861 Renan examined some of these synagogues in Upper Galilee, and was able, for the first time, to decipher the inscriptions correctly.[1] Some years later, two English scholars, Wilson and Anderson,[2] inspected several synagogues in Upper and Lower Galilee on behalf of the Palestine Exploration Fund and partly excavated some of them in the hope of being able to determine the general plan of these structures. In 1872–8 Conder and Kitchener continued the work.[3] But as the excavations were incomplete, they arrived at conclusions which subsequent investigations proved to be incorrect. It is to them, however, that we are indebted for the first drawings and photographs of these remains, by which a knowledge of them was rendered accessible to wider circles. In 1870 the French scholar V. Guérin[4] discovered the remains of some synagogues in other parts of Galilee, which until then had been unknown, but which are found mentioned in the works of the medieval Jewish Pilgrims. Afterwards Sir Laurence Oliphant[5] and G. Schumacher[6] discovered remains of ancient synagogues in Transjordania.

Up to the present the most important work in this field has been done by the Deutsche Orient-Gesellschaft. In

[1] E. Renan, *Mission de Phénicie*, Paris, 1864, pp. 761 ff., Pl. LXX.

[2] C. W. Wilson, 'Notes on Jewish Synagogues in Galilee', *PEF. Q. St.*, 1869, pp. 37 ff.; later in Wilson and Warren, *The Recovery of Jerusalem*, New York, 1871, pp. 267 ff.; and a reprint of the original report in *The Survey of Western Palestine, Special Papers*, London, 1881, pp. 294 ff.

[3] Kitchener, 'Synagogues of Galilee', *PEF. Q. St.*, 1878, pp. 123 ff., and *Survey of Western Palestine, Special Papers*, London, 1881, pp. 299 ff.

[4] *Description de la Palestine, Galilée*, Paris, 1880, vol. i, p. 359, vol. ii, p. 93 f., p. 442 f.

[5] 'Explorations north-east of Lake Tiberias and in Jaulan', *PEF. Q. St.*, 1885, pp. 82 ff.; 'New Discoveries', ibid. 1886, pp. 73 ff.

[6] 'Beschreibung des Dscholan', *ZDPV*, 1886, pp. 278 ff.; pp. 358 ff.

1903 this society sent out two of its members, Hölscher and Thiersch, to Palestine and Phoenicia with a view to selecting sites for excavation. Among other things these scholars drew the attention of the Society to the condition of these ruins, and pointed out that in view of the rapidity with which they were decaying it was necessary to start a thorough exploration without delay. This work was undertaken in 1905 and 1907 by H. Kohl, E. Hiller, and C. Watzinger, who excavated eleven synagogues, two of them in Transjordania. These operations brought to light many interesting details, preliminary reports on which appeared in *Mitteilungen der Deutschen Orient-Gesellschaft*, 27 and 29. To Kohl and Watzinger are due the first exact plans of the monuments. A comprehensive account of their excavations was published in a book entitled *Antike Synagogen in Galiläa* (Leipzig, 1916), a very important work, in which they give an accurate description of the synagogues and their architectural and ornamental features and assign to them their proper place in the history of architecture.

But even these excavations were not complete. The German scholars concentrated mainly upon determining the plan of the synagogues themselves, and in many cases they limited their excavations to a diagonal section sufficient to enable them to reconstruct the plan of the Synagogue proper, and paid no attention to the remainder of the synagogue premises. Of the sites which they excavated, only two have thus far been completely exposed. One was the famous synagogue of Capernaum, situated on property of the Franciscan Order, who in the course of many years brought the work of the German archaeologists to completion.[1] The other is the neighbouring synagogue of Chorazin. Here a hut belonging to some Bedouins had prevented the Germans from excavating the part of the synagogue that was buried underneath it. In 1926 the Department of Antiquities of the Palestine Government expropriated the site and removed this obstacle, exposed

[1] G. Orfali, *Capharnaüm et ses ruines*, Paris, 1922.

the entire synagogue, and brought many important items
of synagogue ornaments and accessories to light.[1]

Since the Great War many other important discoveries
in this field have come to light. As some of these will be
dealt with in fuller detail in a later chapter, they need only
be enumerated here. An interesting synagogue near
Jericho, with the remains of a mosaic floor, was excavated
by the Dominican Fathers of the École Biblique, Jerusalem.[2]
Another synagogue near Tiberias was excavated by the
Jewish Archaeological Society, Jerusalem.[3] In 1929 the
Archaeological Department of the Hebrew University,
Jerusalem, excavated the remains upon which some workers
had chanced in the post-war Jewish settlement of Beth
Alpha in the Valley of Esdraelon.[4] In the same year
another synagogue was discovered in Transjordania in the
ancient city of Gerasa by the Joint Expedition of the Yale
University and the British School of Archaeology.[5] All these
discoveries have contributed a great deal towards clearing
up the problems which exist in connexion with the ancient
synagogues, and have considerably enlarged our knowledge
concerning them. In the course of a survey of the sites of
the old excavations, the Archaeological Department of the
Hebrew University fortuitously discovered some important

[1] A detailed account is in course of preparation by the Archaeological Department of the Hebrew University, Jerusalem.

[2] L. H. Vincent, 'Le Sanctuaire juif d'Ain Douq', RB, 1919, pp.
532 ff.; RB, 1921, p. 442 f.; L. H. Vincent et B. Carrière, 'La Synagogue
de Noarah', RB, 1921, pp. 579 ff.

[3] N. Slouschz, 'The Excavations of the Society at Hama-Tiberias',
in Qobeṣ (Journal of the Jewish Palestine Exploration Society, in
Hebrew), Jerusalem, i, 1921, pp. 5 ff., 1925, pp. 49 ff.

[4] E. L. Sukenik, 'The Ancient Synagogue at Beth-Alpha', Prelimi-
nary Report, Tarbiz (in Hebrew), vol. i, Book 2 (1930), pp. 111 ff.;
The Ancient Synagogue of Beth Alpha (Hebrew and English editions),
Jerusalem-Oxford, 1932.

[5] Crowfoot and Hamilton, 'The Discovery of a Synagogue at Jerash',
PEF. Q. St., 1929, pp. 211 ff.; J. W. Crowfoot, Churches at Jerash
(British School of Archaeology in Jerusalem, Supplementary Papers 3),
London, 1931, pp. 16 ff.

parts of ornaments and inscriptions belonging to ancient synagogues, as well as remains of other synagogues whose existence had previously been unknown. All the points at which remains of ancient synagogues have been found to date are indicated on the map (Plate XIX).

3. *The Synagogue at Capernaum.*

Let us begin with a description of one of the best preserved synagogues that have been found in Palestine until now. On the northern shore of the Sea of Gennesareth, about three kilometres west of the mouth of the Jordan, are the ruins of a Jewish village called by the Arabs Tell-Ḥûm, which is undoubtedly a corruption of Tanḥûm.[1] The identification of this spot was long a subject of controversy, but it may now be accepted as certain that it is the site of the famous Capernaum mentioned in Josephus, the New Testament, the Talmud, and later texts.[2]

Among the many ruins of this city, most of which are of black basalt, there is one of white limestone which has been known for a long time. Jewish tradition, which had forgotten the identity of such sacred remains but not the fact that they were sacred, regarded the spot as the resting-place of several of the Naḥûms and Tanḥûms that have become immortal in Jewish history. One Jewish writer of the early nineteenth century relates that there were wonderful buildings here, from which the present inhabitants of the neighbourhood obtained beautiful dressed stones and transported them to other places to be used for building.[3]

In 1865 Wilson exposed a section of this structure. When he ceased operations, the looting of the stones went on more actively than ever. The Franciscan Order in 1894 earned the gratitude of all friends of Palestine antiquities

---

[1] Capernaum means 'Village of Naḥûm', and Tanḥûm is simply a very common variant of Naḥûm.

[2] Capernaum is mentioned in one of the mosaic inscriptions of the recently discovered Synagogue in Ḥammath-by-Gadara.

[3] *Ḥibbath Yerushalayim*, p. 23.

by purchasing the ruin from its Bedouin owners and covering it up effectively with earth.

That this synagogue was among those which were explored intensively by Kohl and Watzinger, whose work was completed by the Franciscan Fathers, has already been related. In 1925 the Order received the permission of the Department of Antiquities to restore parts of the synagogue, which operations were carried out by the late Father Gaudentius Orfali (see Pl. I).

Facing the sea, the two-storied white structure, contrasting vividly with the black basalt round about, was no doubt an imposing sight. The ground-plan of the synagogue is that of a rectangle 20·40 metres long by 18·65 metres broad (Fig. 1). It is orientated southward (with an eastward inclination of 15 degrees) towards Jerusalem. On the east side there is a courtyard, the shape of a trapezium, running along the whole length of the synagogue. In front of the building (south) is a platform, to which a flight of steps leads up from the east and from the west. At the northwest corner is an annex of a small square chamber; staircases on the eastern and western sides lead up to its roof, and thence to the gallery of the synagogue proper. On the west side of the synagogue runs a street about 4 metres wide paved with basalt stones. The foundations are of basalt, but the upper courses of the walls are of limestone. The walls, which are 60 or 70 centimetres thick, are divided on the outside into several fields by pilasters. The western wall, which has no doors, has nine pilasters, the northern wall five, the eastern again nine, and the southern four. Each pilaster stands upon a plinth and an Attic base, and was crowned with a simple capital of fillet, ovolo, and cavetto.

The spaces between the pilasters are not equal, but the pilasters themselves measure almost uniformly from 59 to 60 cm. in width and 3 cm. in thickness on every side of the building. Of the entablature of these rows of pilasters only remnants of a simple sima have been found both inside and outside the building. Apparently the pilasters were joined above their capitals by this sima, a duplicate of which ran along the inner face of the wall at the same height above the ground.

The façade of the synagogue is on the south looking towards Jerusalem. The four pilasters divide it into a wide

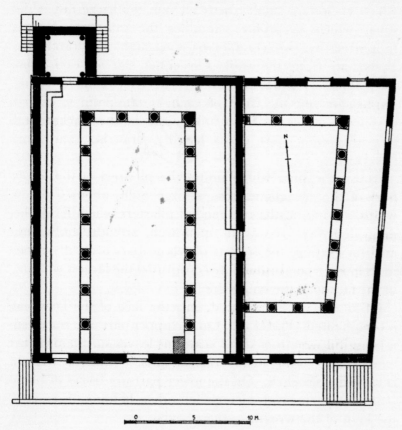

Fig. 1. CAPERNAUM, PLAN OF SYNAGOGUE.

middle and two narrow lateral fields. The middle field contains the main doorway and each of the others is provided with a smaller entrance.

The Main Doorway (1·77 m. wide). Of this the threshold, with two sockets for the two door-wings, is still in place. A frame, divided into three fasciae surrounded by ovolo and cavetto, rose from the doorposts to the lintel, in the middle

of which it was interrupted by a relief, of which only traces
of an eagle with outspread wings remain. From the same
stone was hewn the frieze, of the sculpture of which six
Erotes, their bodies effaced except for the wings, are still
discernible. The Erotes are carrying five garlands, each of
which encloses a small rosette. Upon the frieze rested the
sima, which in profile resembles the pilasters. It was
supported by two consoles 65 cm. high and projecting
25–30 cm. from the wall. On either side of each con-
sole, along its entire length, are carved two intertwining
spirals, and on the front of each a date-palm is carved
in relief, complete with trunk (clear of the background
for the greater part of its length), branches, and fruit
(Pl. II *a*).

Above the sima which unites the pilasters of the lower
part of the synagogue, rose a large arch, about 6 m. in
width, resting on the two medial pilasters which flank the
main doorway. It was an open arch, provided only with
an iron grating, the sockets of whose bars are still visible
in its lower face. It therefore constituted the largest window
in the façade of the synagogue.

Of all the voussoirs found, only the face of the keystone
is ornamented (Pl. III *a*). On the upper part of it is carved
a beautiful wreath of small acanthus leaves surmounted by
a flower and ending in a Heraclean knot. Within the wreath
is carved a sea-shell. On the lower part are traces of birds
(eagles?), their heads facing each other, holding the ends of
the knot of the wreath in their beaks.

The *Side Doorways* were 1·40 m. wide. The doorposts
consisted of pilasters resting upon Attic bases and surmounted by ornamented lintels. The lintel of the east
doorway has been preserved almost intact, but its ornamentation has been entirely obliterated. Its face was divided
horizontally into two unequal fields. In the lower field,
which is the larger one, there are unmistakable traces of
figures, apparently of centaurs, in the midst of five date-
palms. Slight traces indicate that the upper part of the

field was occupied by an eagle with drooping wings. The lintel is bordered by a row of acanthus leaves on the moulded frieze above.

The lintel of the west doorway, which is likewise divided into two fields, is in a much worse condition. In the middle of this lintel there is a crater, the remaining part being divided by palm-trees into fields occupied by animal figures, now completely effaced. The upper field was surmounted by a moulded frieze of vine branches issuing from two craters at the two ends of the lintel. As the remains of this lintel show, it excelled by its fine workmanship.

Windows of the Façade. Above the arch opened a window 102 cm. high by 80 cm. wide, of which sundry remains were found both on the inside and on the outside. It was provided with an iron grating, as is evident from the sockets in the sill and in the sides. On each of the sides of the window, which are 50 cm. deep, are two small columns diagonally fluted, with Attic bases and Corinthian capitals. The window was crowned with a pediment having a shell in its centre and ivy and tendrils respectively above its two acroteria. There were probably two more windows in the upper part of the house to light the gallery, and there may have been others below as well, above each of the side doorways, to light the aisles.

A frieze and a cornice, many parts of which were found among the ruins in front of the south side of the synagogue, completed the upper part of the façade.

Some of the ornamented stones found were voussoirs, showing that the line of the frieze was interrupted in the middle by an arch, corresponding to the window-arch above the main doorway. The ornamentation of the frieze begins below with a smooth narrow band, above that is a slightly raised ovolo, and above the ovolo acanthus leaves from which figures of lions emerge; these have been deliberately effaced (Pl. III b). From the position of the leaves and the posture of the animals, which on some of the stones face to the right and on others to the left, it may be inferred that two wreaths started from the two ends of the frieze and joined in the centre.

The cornice above this frieze is decorated with strings of eggs, a dentil band, and a Lesbian cyma, and above them protrudes a plate ornamented with astragal; in its lower part rosettes alternate with consoles.

The parts of the pediment, whose ornamentation is similar to that of the cornice, are supplemented by a sima on which palmettes alternate with acanthus leaves.

The East Side. On the east side, before which was a court containing a portico, there was only one entrance to the synagogue. The lintel of this doorway, 80 cm. in height, is broken into two unequal parts. A broad guilloche encloses the whole face of the lintel in a rectangular frame and also divides it vertically into three almost equal fields. In the two lateral fields are carved, within rectangular frames, flowers of diverse execution, of nine petals each, flanked on either side by erect acanthus leaves. In the centre of the middle field are two concentric wreaths from which bands go out in various directions.

A window-sill which was found in the neighbourhood, with sockets for bars and for the insertion of window-posts, no doubt formed part of a window which opened above the entrance we have been describing. No other traces of windows have been found on this side.

The North Side. No entrance to the synagogue was found on the north side. In the nave of the synagogue was found a window-post (102 cm. high by 142 cm. broad) resembling the parts of the window found on the south side in its ornamentation. It apparently belongs to a window which opened on this side from the women's gallery.

At the west end of this side, a small square structure joined on to the main building, with which it was connected by a small door. Its roof was supported by four pillars of limestone. Women mounted to their gallery by means of basalt staircases leaning against the east and west sides of this structure. In the clearing of this room, many fragments of glass vessels and large earthen jars were found. These vessels had probably contained oil for the illumination and other uses of the house. This was evidently the store-room of the synagogue.

The West Side. On the west side there was no entrance to the synagogue, notwithstanding one of the streets of the town ran along it. In all probability it lacked windows, perhaps for climatic reasons.

The Interior. The floor of the synagogue, consisting of limestone flags of various sizes (20 to 24 cm. in thickness), rests on a bed of small basalt stones. From the floor rose the stylobate (9–14 cm. high, 89 cm. wide) at a distance of 3·56 m. from the east and west walls and 2·27 m. from the north side. It divided the interior of the synagogue into a broad nave (8·38 m. wide) and three narrow side aisles. On the east and west sides, two benches were built one above the other, coterminous with the walls. Each bench was 43–6 cm. high and 54–6 cm. wide. The stones of the benches taper downwards for the greater comfort of the occupants' legs (Pl. IV *a*). In the south-west corner there is still in place a rounded piece of the upper bench provided with a back carved out of the stone, which is decorated in front with the relief of a head with dishevelled hair. Perhaps this was a seat of honour in the synagogue. The walls above the benches were plastered with distemper of various colours and perhaps stuccoed. Small quantities of coloured distemper have been found among the ruins.

The columns did not rest immediately upon the stylobate but on rectangular pedestals, most of them being still *in situ.* There were seven columns on each of the long sides (east and west) and two between the northernmost columns of each row. The two corner pedestals differed in form from the others. The inner angles of their square bodies were cut away, thus forming two half pedestals, and the bases which rested above, as well as the shafts of the columns, were heart-shaped.

The diameter of the columns is 62 cm. below and 58 cm. above, and their height is 3·76 metres.

The capitals are Corinthian. A row of miniature acanthus leaves marks the lower border, and above it rise, one above the other, two rows of large acanthus leaves, eight to each row, each leaf of the upper row rising out of the space between two leaves in the lower. From the upper row volutes go out to the four edges of the abacus, together with smaller medial volutes, above which the abacus is ornamented with a flower.

Eighteen parts of the entablature above the colonnade have been found within and outside the walls. The epistyle was divided into three fasciae separated by a fillet and finished with ovolo and cavetto; and above them was another smooth broad ovolo like a kind of frieze. In the soffit is engraved a cavetto in the shape of a Lesbian cyma, which serves as a frame to a narrow strip that projects to the same plane as the surface of the stone. In the back of the stones which were found whole, there are four square hollows which used to hold the ends of the wooden beams whose other ends rested on the walls of the house.

Upon this epistyle rested another sima, of which likewise a large number of pieces were found. Its profile resembles in every respect that of the sima which joined the pilasters on the outer side of the walls.

These parts enable a calculation of the height of the lateral aisles that surrounded the nave on three sides:

stylobate and pedestal . . .	approximately 1·30 m.
columns	,, 3·75 m.
capitals	,, 0·70 m.
epistyle (less the holes designed for the beams)	,, 0·67 m.
	approximately 6·42 m.

The existence of upper rows of columns and a gallery, which rested upon the lower columns, is proved by the presence among the ruins of the synagogue of columns and capitals different from those described above.

Most of the upper columns have been removed too, and it is only by means of a surviving fragment of a corner column (1·65 m. long), which apparently stood in the north-west corner, that we are able to infer that it tapered upwards (diameter at the base 52·5 cm., at the capital 49 cm.) and that it was 10 cm. narrower than the lower columns. The top part of a shaft with its capital, both carved out of one and the same stone, was found near the fragment in question and evidently belonged to the same column. The capital is similar in every respect to those of the outer pilasters, consisting of ovolo and cavetto surmounted by an abacus. The other capitals of this sort which were found are of the same form. As no bases that can be assigned to this row of columns have been found, it would seem that they stood immediately on the entablature above the lower rows.

The epistyle of the upper rows is smaller than that of the lower ones (0·76 m. high). Three fasciae, separated by a Lesbian cyma, are wrought in ovolo and cavetto.

On the soffit are the same depression and protruding band, and in addition every stone is provided with hollows for the ends of the wooden beams. Above this, there were apparently only the rafters. The height of the gallery is difficult to determine, as there is not a single whole upper column left; 3·50 m. will not be far from the truth.

Numerous pieces of masonry pertaining to wall architecture, such as pilasters, bases, capitals and friezes which were found in the debris, give some idea of the peculiar ornamentation of the walls of the gallery.

The pilasters have Attic bases and Corinthian capitals. From the many parts of pilasters and capitals found, it may be inferred with certainty that the upper walls on the east and on the west were decorated with such pilasters. It is not known, on the other hand, whether the north wall was so ornamented.

No remains of an epistyle of the pilasters have been found. Evidently the frieze was in immediate contact with them. Many parts of the frieze have been found, including some with projecting sections. These projections rested directly upon the capitals.

Below the frieze is a narrow blank border, and above, likewise carved out of the same stone, is the cornice, consisting, from below upwards, of egg-and-dart, dentil band, astragal, and a broader strip of alternating acanthus leaves and palmettes. The main motive of the frieze is a circle of acanthus stalks and leaves. The latter, four in number, lie tip to base and are orientated in the opposite circular direction to those of the neighbouring design. The veins of the stalks stand out sharply. The enclosed space is occupied by various embellishments.

In contrast to the external frieze of the façade, representations of the animal kingdom are wanting among these ornaments. Their place is taken by motives from the vegetable kingdom and sundry geometrical figures such as the pentagram and the hexagram. Only the stones of the north frieze, which differed from the others in their ornamentation, bear traces of figures, which, however, were later effaced like the other figures that originally graced the synagogue.

A few stones from among this number are described below and illustrated in the photographs. One of the stones (Pl. IV b) has on its frieze, from left to right, a flower composed of five acanthus leaves, a hexagram, a six-petalled star-shaped rosette inscribed in a hexagon of leaves, and a five-petalled flower. The cornice of this stone is badly damaged. Another stone, on which both frieze and cornice are well preserved (Pl. V a), displays a flower of seven whirling petals which are folded in the opposite circular direction to the leaves of the acanthus ring, a five-petalled flower, three clusters of grapes and three pomegranates.

Further mention should be made of the stones which rested on the pilaster capitals. They are considerably damaged, but the restorations in the sketches are quite certain. They are decorated with reliefs of a heptagram with Amazons' targes between its points, a sunflower, an amphora with two clusters of grapes hanging down, a hexa-petalon with all of its members folded clockwise, another with its members folded counter-clockwise, respectively (Pl. VI).

As previously stated, there were no representations of animals on the friezes of the east and west walls of the gallery, but the ornamentation of a few other frieze-stones, belonging, to judge from their location in the ruins, to the north wall, differs from that of the preceding.

Here the frieze and cornice stones were separate from each other. On one of the stones of the cornice, the sima after the half palmette at its end is adorned with two eagles, their backs turned to each other and the tips of their tails practically touching, but looking backwards at each other and holding the two ends of a garland in their beaks (Pl. V b). To their right is portrayed a sea-horse with its tail bent forward and a broad girdle in the middle of its body; a broad horn stands out from its head, and it has a goat's beard; one foreleg is stretched forward, and its head is turned backward.[1] Part of an acanthus leaf at the other end indicates that this ornament ended here and the motive of alternating palmettes and acanthus leaves was resumed. Of the frieze stones, one, which may have been situated in the centre of this wall, is particulary interesting (Pl. V c). At its end is carved a carriage in the shape of a small temple standing on wheels, of which only two are visible.[2]

[1] Precisely the same motives are employed on the Menorah which Titus brought back to Rome from the pillaged Temple of Jerusalem. Cf. below, p. 63.

[2] So far this unique piece of sculpture has not been explained in a satisfactory manner. Watzinger (op. cit., pp. 193 ff.) explains it as the Roman carruca (קרובין in the Talmud) reserved for conveying princes and other dignities. He says further that the carruca having been one of the privileges of the house of R. Juda han-Nasi, it was introduced in the decoration of the synagogue in order to commemorate this

All these mural decorations, although in the upper part of the gallery, were visible to those below in the synagogue.

The Ark. In the interior of the nave, before the south wall, were found various carved stones belonging to some interior structure, without doubt the Ark of the Scrolls of the Law, which stood before the south wall, the side which is towards Jerusalem.

The remains show that there were two shells, next to each other, above the openings of the Ark. From one of them which has remained intact, we see that the width of the opening was 74 cm. Of the other shell only two fragments have been preserved. The shell proper and the frieze above it are carved out of one stone. The ornamentation of this

privilege granted to the head of Jewry. A further reason for this explanation is according to him the fact that this frieze belongs to the north wall, opposite the Ark, where there was also the seat of the head of the community, so that the representation of the *carruca* appeared above his chair. This theory, accepted by several scholars, does not appeal to us, as it did not appeal to others in the past (e.g. S. Cook, *Religion of Ancient Palestine*, Schweich Lectures for 1925, London, 1930, p. 214 f.). This privilege must have been appreciated by the contemporary Jewry, but it is very doubtful whether they would have considered it of sufficient importance to permanently commemorate it in the synagogue. On the other hand, the explanation of this *carruca* as a portable shrine seems to be even less based on facts. It is true that the Ark occasionally used to be taken out of doors, but it is never mentioned as having been transported on wheels, nor do we find wheels attached to any of the numerous arks depicted on mosaic floors, lintels, gilt glass dishes, &c. The only occasion on which we find a chariot mentioned in connexion with Jewish religious conception is the vision of Ezekiel (Ezek. chs. 1, 10). Without pressing the point at all, I should like to call the attention to two facts: (*a*) that Capernaum was the seat of mystics and sectarians (מינים *Eccles. Rabba*, 1, 8) who, to a certain degree, might have influenced the ideas of the orthodox community; (*b*) that this is the only synagogue with representations of pentagrams, hexagrams, and heptagrams, which certainly have the value of magic symbols. The fact that the chariot was represented in the form of a contemporary vehicle cannot invalidate this suggestion; the sculptor has simply chosen the finest and most honoured type of a chariot as his model. But I repeat that I do not want to press this point.

frieze is very similar to that of the façade: between half-wreaths of acanthus leaves are discernible the foreparts of figures of animals which have been deliberately defaced. The same motives are repeated on the frieze which extends beyond the shells on both sides. The frieze was surmounted by a cornice, which also crowned the shells in the shape of arches. The two shells were surmounted by a pediment.

To the structure of the Ark, no doubt, belong two statues of lions of which remains were found during the excavations.

The construction of the Ark, which occupied almost the entire width of the nave, rendered the main entrance impracticable. It evidently formed no part of the original plan of the synagogue, and the conclusions to be drawn from this fact are dealt with on p. 52.

The Courtyard and Terrace adjoining the Synagogue. On the east side of the house was the trapezoid court which extended along its entire length. Its width at the north end was 13·34 m. and at the south end only 11·26 m.

A portico surrounded three sides of the court, its width being 3·50 m. on the south side, 3·24 on the east, and about 2·5 m. on the north. Most of the court therefore remained exposed. The columns stood upon a stylobate 84 cm. wide. As inside the synagogue, the columns did not stand immediately upon the stylobate but upon pedestals about 1·20 m. high. The pedestals are, apart from minor differences in measurements, just like those inside. On the north and on the south, where the rows of columns touched the east wall of the synagogue, the half-columns were not inserted into the wall but built against it. At the north-east and south-east corners, there were also double columns.

These columns were crowned with Corinthian capitals. To judge by those which remain, the capitals were not all of the same form and were inferior in workmanship to those of the columns inside.

On one corner capital (Pl. VII *a*) which was found next to the double column on the south side, two terminal volutes issue above two rows of superficially engraved

acanthus leaves without any visible connexion with the
acanthus stalks. The medial caliculi are entirely wanting,
and in their stead a six-pointed star rises in the centre.
Different from this corner capital in its ornaments is the
interesting capital (55 cm. high) discovered in the latest
excavations, which bears on its four sides an olive branch,
a pomegranate, a wreath (Pl. VII *b*), and a seven-branched
candlestick (Pl. VII *c*) similar to the one which was found
depicted on a capital from the synagogue of Ḥammath-by-
Tiberias. This capital too seems to have belonged to the
colonnade in the court.

The cornice of the colonnade in the court consisted of an
epistyle, 85 cm. high by 66 cm. broad, of which many parts
have been found. As no vestiges of a frieze were found, it
may be inferred that the roof of the portico rested directly
upon this epistyle.

The latest excavations of the Franciscans have brought
to light several lintels of gates to this court. Father Orfali
concludes that eight gates opened into this courtyard, two
on the south, three on the east, and three on the north.
Only three of the lintels can be assigned with certainty to
definite gates by comparing their measurements with those
of the gates discovered. The others are assigned according
to the places where they were found. It is hard to under-
stand why there were three gates on the east side, where
the ground is very sloping and the approach inconvenient.
Of the main gate, which led into the courtyard from the
south, a lintel 2·46 m. long and 64 cm. broad was found.
The lintel is well preserved (Pl. II *b*). Part of its face is
occupied by a frame with three fasciae, no doubt a continua-
tion of the dressing of the doorposts; in the centre is a relief
of an Ark of the Law. To the right of this is a rosette and
to the left a palm branch and a garland. The upper part is
rounded off to the right of the Ark by a row of elongated
eggs set in rings and to the left by acanthus leaves in the
shape of palmettes.

The lintel of the other entrance on the same side, which

was about 1·25 m. wide, is badly damaged. One can still distinguish on it a twisted rope and traces of leaves, over which hangs a garland.

The three gates on the east were about 5·60 m. apart. The outer side of some fragments of gate-posts from these openings is divided into three fasciae surrounded by ovolo and cavetto.

On one of the stones of a gate-post, which apparently belonged to the middle gate of this side, is carved a capital, in whose lower half stands an acanthus leaf in the form of a palmette flanked by half a leaf of the same species on either side, the whole overhung by a row of egg-and-dart. A small vine tendril ending in volutes completes the ornamentation of the capital.

The face of the lintel is divided by a vine-branch, complete with leaves and clusters, into three fields. It seems that these were occupied by representations of living creatures which have been completely destroyed (Pl. II c).

The court, like the interior, was paved with large slabs of stone. In the remaining parts of the enclosing wall pilasters project from the stones, and perhaps, like the walls of the synagogue proper, it was divided by them into several fields.

In front of the façade, where the ground is sloping, a terrace 3·30 m. wide was built along the whole width of the synagogue. The terrace too was paved with smoothed slabs of stone. Near the outer edge of the terrace a strip about 40 cm. wide remained unsmoothed. Apparently a balustrade of some sort resting on this part bordered the entire length of the terrace. The staircases are at the east and west ends of the terrace. At the west end there are only four steps, about 3·55 m. long each; but on the east side, owing to the steep gradient, many more were required.

4. *The Synagogue at Chorazin* (Fig. 2).

An hour's climb above Capernaum (Tell Ḥûm) lies Chorazin (Kerâze), whose synagogue ruin may be briefly

described by way of supplement to the foregoing. This is
the other site which, as already mentioned, was partly
excavated by the German expedition. In 1926 it was
completely cleared by the Department of Antiquities of the
Palestine Government. The synagogue, which faces south,
is a structure about 20 m. long and 13 m. wide, divided
by two rows of columns into a nave 6·60 m. wide and
two aisles each 3·20 m. wide (Pl. VIII a). At the north end,
as at Capernaum, the two longitudinal rows of columns are
joined by a transverse one, leaving a third north aisle
3·50 m. in width. In the façade are the usual three entrances
into the three longitudinal divisions of the basilica. The
later excavations revealed the fact that several terraces,
connected by steps, were built upon the sloping ground in
front of the building leading up to a platform on top, on
which probably stood a portico, and that there were two
annexes on the west side of the basilica. The smaller and
more northern of these chambers contains a staircase, which
of course mounted to the women's gallery. There was very
probably a court on the east side. Several courses of the
west wall are still *in situ*; and as the annexes were on this
side they are only roughly hewn and were no doubt covered
over with distemper. On the east and north sides the single
surviving upper course shows much better workmanship
(Pl. VIII b).

Unlike the Capernaum synagogue, that of Chorazin was
built of the local stone: basalt. The many fragments of
scattered masonry allow a fairly exact reconstruction of
the façade. Like that of Capernaum, it had an arched
window above the main portal and was crowned by a gabled
roof. A great number of wrought stones also afford a good
idea of the interior decoration of the synagogue. As in
Capernaum, the walls of the gallery were decorated with
a frieze displaying various motives of geometrical patterns
and human and animal figures. Though the fallen basalt
stones are naturally split and chipped, it is quite certain
that no deliberate mutilation has been perpetrated here.

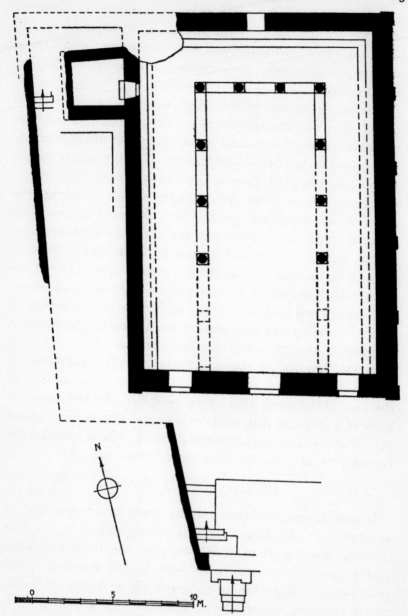

FIG. 2. CHORAZIN, SKETCH-PLAN OF SYNAGOGUE.

From the location in which they were found, it is evident that the stones carved with animal figures belong to the west and north walls, the east one, as the later excavations showed, having been ornamented with geometrical and floral designs.

The workmanship of the reliefs in the synagogue of this out-of-the-way little community, executed upon a not very compact variety of basalt, is naturally greatly inferior to that found in near-by Capernaum. The figures are mostly framed in vine branches or acanthus leaves. On one of the stones we see, from left to right, a man standing with a rod in his raised right hand and a cluster of grapes in his lowered left; a man standing on the left and a woman sitting on the right, a cluster of grapes hanging above them; a woman and a man sitting, the latter with arm outstretched to an overhanging cluster of grapes. On another stone, a Medusa head is quite clearly visible; on still another, an animal suckling her two whelps; on a fourth, considerably chipped, a struggle between a centaur and a lion.

In the interior of the synagogue, several fragments of miniature architecture point to the existence of an Ark of the Law at the south wall. To it no doubt also belonged the body of a lion and fragments of a second which were found. For an account of the inscribed *kathedra*, which was likewise brought to light by the later excavations, see p. 60.

5. *The Synagogue at Kafr Bir'im.*

In conclusion, mention may be made of a synagogue in another part of Galilee which is distinguished by the fact that the lower part of its façade, with the three doorways and a part of the portico as well, is still standing. The synagogue of Kafr Bir'im measures 18·10 m. by 13·95 m. and is directed to the south. Like the two preceding it is divided by two longitudinal and one transverse row of columns into a nave and three aisles. The width of the nave is 6·20 m.; that of the two lateral aisles 2·85 m. and that of the north one 2·14 m. The portico in front is 4 m. wide.

The façade would not seem to have been ornamented like
that of the synagogues previously described, its main feature
being the three doorways. The middle one, topped by an
arch, is quite graceful (see Frontispiece). In the centre of
its lintel is a wreath flanked by two figures which have been
deliberately effaced. This is exactly the same motive as

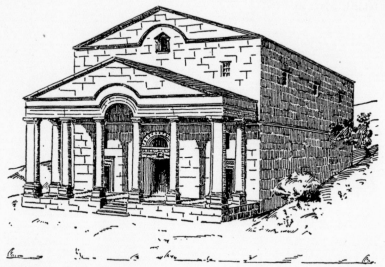

FIG. 3. KAFR BIR'IM, restoration of synagogue after Kohl and Watzinger.

that of the lintel of the other now completely obliterated
synagogue of Kafr Bir'im which we shall have occasion
to refer to again (v. p. 70). The two figures were at first
supposed to have been pascal lambs, but as Watzinger[1] has
shown, they are more likely to have been hovering genii
holding the wreath in their hands. A similar motive appears
on a lintel of the synagogue in ed-Dikkeh in Transjordania
and on another one recently discovered in er-Râmeh, north
of Acre. The cornice, consisting of a vine-branch issuing
from an amphora, is made of the same stone as the body
of the lintel.

An idea of the architecture of this synagogue can be
obtained from the reconstruction shown in Fig. 3.

[1] Op. cit., p. 199 f.

E

In the masonry of the peasants' dwellings in Kafr Bir'im, the writer some years ago located stones with signs of the zodiac carved upon them in relief, as well as the head of a statue of a lion, both originally from the ancient synagogues of the village.[1]

[1] E. L. Sukenik, *The Ancient Synagogue of Beth Alpha*, Jerusalem-Oxford, 1932, pp. 33, 57.

CHAPTER II

IN the development of synagogue architecture in Palestine, two stages can be distinguished. In the earlier type
of synagogue, the Ark of the Law was not permanently
stationed in the main hall, and accordingly there was no
receptacle in the wall of the hall for this purpose (*v.* p. 52).
As therefore the side facing Jerusalem, where the Ark was
placed when it was brought into the basilica, was thus
occupied only during a part of the services, the orientation
was emphasized by the façade with its doors. Consequently,
when the custom was later introduced of building a
stationary Ark on this side, the main entrance was blocked
(*v.* p. 53). In the new type of synagogue we accordingly
find an apse for the Ark in the wall facing Jerusalem, and
the doors in the opposite wall.

Another feature which distinguished the new type from
the old was the employment of mosaics instead of flagstones
in the floors. At Umm al-'Amad (in the Sahl el-Baṭṭôf,
called Biq'ath Beth Neṭopha in the Talmud), one of the
places excavated by the German expedition in 1905–6,
remains of a plain mosaic floor were found over an older
one of flagstones.[1] A few mosaic inscriptions were, however,
found before the Great War at Kafr Kanna[2] and Sepphoris.[3]
After the war, whole synagogues paved with mosaic were
discovered, and revealed a cycle of designs peculiar to such
edifices. By a piece of good fortune, we now possess reliable
literary evidence as well for the date at which this custom
was introduced. A fragment of the Palestinian Talmud,
Aboda Zara, 41d 1. 37–42 a 1. 7, in the State Library at
Leningrad, published by J. N. Epstein in *Tarbiz*, iii. 19,
pp. 15 ff., contains the following line, which has dropped out
of our ordinary text through homoeoteleuton: ביומי דר' אבון
שרון ציירין על פסיפסס (ψήφωσις) ולא מחי בידון 'In the days of

[1] Kohl and Watzinger, op. cit., p. 145 f.
[2] Clermont-Ganneau in *PEF. Q. St.*, 1901, p. 251; ibid., pp. 374 ff.
[3] Id., in *CAIL*, 1909, pp. 677 ff.

R. Abun they began to depict designs on mosaics, and he did not hinder them.'

This R. Abun is known to have lived in the first half of the fourth century. It should be explained that 'depict designs' must mean here 'make representations of living creatures'; for there could not have been any doubt about the propriety of pictorial representations of other objects, in view of their frequency both before and after this date. Perhaps at the time this concession was only taken advantage of in private homes, and pictures of animal life may not have found their way into synagogues until even later; but at any rate the first half of the fourth century is the *terminus a quo*. Certainly the synagogue mosaics of this sort that have thus far come to light are not earlier than the fifth century.

1. *Na'aran*.

The first complete mosaic floor of a synagogue to be discovered in our days was that at 'Ain Dûk (*v*. p. 6, n. 2), the Biblical Na'aran, near Jericho, which was excavated in 1921 by the École Biblique et Archéologique Française of the Dominicans in Jerusalem. The building here too, although having its doors on the north side, faces south. It consists of a courtyard, vestibule, and basilica, the latter with an annex on its south-west corner (Fig. 4). The last three are all paved with mosaic floors. In the vestibule the design consists of a seven-branched candlestick, 2·40 m. long, in various colours. It is surmounted by an inscription and lies in the middle of another (*v*. p. 75). The interior of the main hall, 21 m. by 14·80 m., was divided by two rows of pillars into a nave and two aisles. Its mosaic was richly ornamented. That of the nave is divided into four transverse panels with inscriptions distributed in various places. The first panel, in front of the entrance, consists of linked polygons, circles, and semicircles. These geometrical figures serve as frames for pictures of beasts and birds and various motives from the vegetable kingdom. The animal and vegetable motives include a hare, a jackal standing between bushes, a pheasant standing on the branch of a tree, clusters of grapes, palm-branches, a basket of fruit, &c. They display quite a finished execution, the colours varying from shiny black, through various shades of blue and green, to

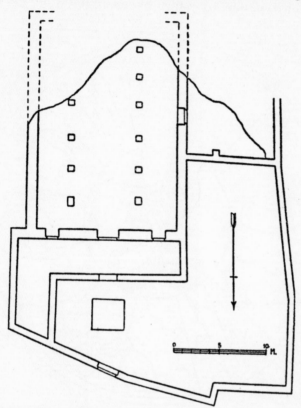

Fig. 4. NA'ARAN, PLAN OF SYNAGOGUE.

several different kinds of white. The mosaicists utilized all the stones of various hues in which this region is so rich.

The second panel contains the cycle of the zodiac, which unfortunately was badly mutilated at a very early date (Fig. 5).

In the centre of the cycle is a figure driving a quadriga, representing the Sun, and round about it are the twelve signs of the zodiac with their Hebrew names. At the four corners of the panel are four figures symbolic of the four

seasons of the year, also with their names. Only the out-
lines of these mutilated figures can still be distinguished,
whereas the inscriptions have been almost perfectly
preserved.

The third panel, to judge by its richness in inscribed

FIG. 5. NA'ARAN, MOSAIC FLOOR, ZODIAC.

blessings (v. p. 73), the most important of all, contains a
picture of two lions approaching from either end towards
a man standing in the centre in an attitude of prayer. The
accompanying legend דניאל שלום leaves no doubt as to the
Biblical situation that was thus portrayed. This was the
first trace of a Jewish cycle of Biblical pictorial motives in
the early centuries of the current era to be discovered.

The fourth panel contains a picture of the Ark of the Law,

flanked by two seven-branched candlesticks, each with two glass lamps hanging from either side (Fig. 6).

At the time when these excavations were made, the data for determining the period of this synagogue were not yet available.

Now, however, the new literary evidence cited above

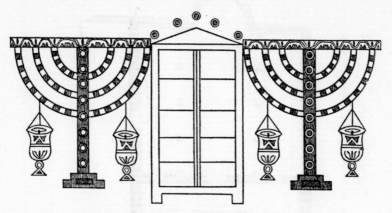

FIG. 6. NA'ARAN, MOSAIC FLOOR. Ark with two candlesticks.

precludes any date prior to the late fourth century, while recent excavations point to the fifth century as more probable.

2. Beth Alpha.

Another synagogue of this type was discovered accidentally in 1928 in the course of drainage operations carried out by the young Jewish settlement of Beth Alpha, in the Valley of Esdraelon, not far from Beisan (v. p. 6). It was excavated by the writer in the following year on behalf of the Hebrew University, Jerusalem, and an area of 28 m. by 14 m. was exposed. It is occupied by the court, vestibule, and basilica of the synagogue, the latter, as at 'Ain Dûk, with an annex on its south-west corner, which, however, is not well preserved (Fig. 7). The building is rather irregular and of poor workmanship. Of interest, however, is the apse projecting from its south wall, which, as already indicated, served as a repository for the Ark of the Law. It was the first to be discovered in Palestine, though the south wall of the 'Ain Dûk synagogue, which is unfortunately washed away, very likely also contained one. The Beth Alpha synagogue was originally provided with stone benches only along three of its walls, but evidently the

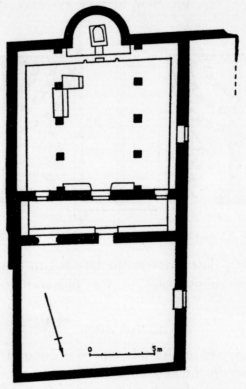

FIG. 7. BETH ALPHA, plan of synagogue.

seating capacity was later found inadequate, and a few benches were placed upon the mosaic at various points. Another afterthought was the *Bema* (*v.* p. 57). The doors are naturally on the north side.

The entire area is paved with mosaic floors. Those of the courtyard, the vestibule, and the aisles display comparatively simple decoration, but that of the nave is extraordinarily rich in colourful and varied, if primitive, pictorial representations (Fig. 8). It is divided into three panels, the

FIG. 8. BETH ALPHA, DIAGRAM OF MAIN MOSAIC FLOOR.

whole enclosed in an ornamental border containing, near the entrance, two inscriptions (see p. 76 f.).

The first panel from the entrance contains a representation of the Sacrifice of Isaac, showing all the dramatis personae advancing from left to right. The farthest behind are naturally the two lads with the ass of which they have been left in charge. At the right end stands the altar with the fire burning upon it. Abraham, an elderly, corpulent greybeard, is standing to the left of it, holding the infant Isaac—whose hands are tied behind him—towards the altar with his left hand and the knife in his right. His head is inclined in a listening attitude and his eyes are turned to the left, presumably looking for something. That which has diverted his attention from the altar is depicted in the centre. Here is seen, above, a radiant cloud, projecting in part beyond the frame of the panel proper, from which projects an open hand;[1] below it is written אל תשלח 'Lay not (thy hand)', *Gen.* 22: 12. Below that is a bush, to which a ram is tied with a cord; next to its head is the legend והנה איל 'and behold a ram', ibid. *v.* 13. Abraham and Isaac also have their names inscribed above them. The rest of the picture, representing the two lads with the ass, is devoid of inscriptions, no doubt because it is removed from the main scene of action.

Above the panel proper is a band of alternating red and black palm-trees, indicative of the landscape.

The middle panel is larger than the other two and nearly square in shape. It is occupied by a representation of the Zodiac. The arrangement is almost identical with that of 'Ain Dûk. The chariot of the Sun is in the centre, the Twelve

---

[1] The hand as the symbol of God's power recurs frequently in early Christian representations of this scene. The figure has its origin in the Bible, where 'the hand', or 'right hand', or 'arm of the Lord' is used very often not only as a metaphor for 'God's power' but also with much the same meaning as just the Divine Name alone. Representations of hands, perhaps with a similar significance, are also found on Punic stelae, Babylonian seal cylinders, &c.

Signs in a circle, and the Four Seasons, here recognizable as winged genii, in the corners of the panel. And also as at 'Ain Dûk, the names of the Signs and the Seasons are inscribed. The whole is in an almost perfect state of preservation.

The third panel, in front of the apse, appropriately contains, like the last panel at 'Ain Dûk, a representation of the Ark and other synagogue appurtenances. They are included in a space from before which a curtain is being drawn to either side in order to expose its contents. In the centre is the Ark of the Law, flanked by two Menorahs and other ritual objects and by two lions.

3. Jerash.

In the same year as Beth Alpha was discovered, another synagogue with a mosaic floor was found at Jerash by the Joint Expedition of the Yale University and the British School of Archaeology, Jerusalem.[1] It was discovered beneath the remains of a Byzantine church in which was found inscribed a date equivalent to 530–1 C.E. The synagogue was accordingly built before that date, apparently in the first half of the fifth century. Whilst the church was orientated to the east, the synagogue that had preceded it faced west, as might be expected in Transjordania. Consequently, the apse of the church coincided roughly with the vestibule of the synagogue (Fig. 9). It was here that the excavators discovered, below the floor of the church, another mosaic belonging to the synagogue. It consists of a long rectangular panel containing a new link in the chain of Biblical scenes in synagogue mosaics; viz. the story of the Flood (Pl. IX). The artistic merit of this picture far surpasses that of any of those hitherto discussed; doubtless because the congregation, in the flourishing city of Gerasa, could afford to employ superior workmen. In the fragment of the mosaic that has survived, there still remain the heads of two men over which are inscribed respectively CHM and IAΦIΘ,

[1] v. p. 6 n. 5.

i.e. Shem and Japhet. The missing part may have contained other members of the family, and the Ark, or perhaps the altar upon which Noah sacrificed upon coming

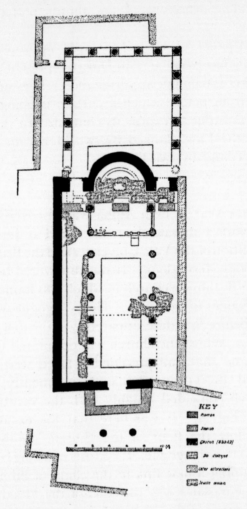

FIG. 9. JERASH, PLAN OF SYNAGOGUE AND LATER CHURCH.
(*By permission of the British School of Archaeology, Jerusalem.*)

out of the Ark. We also see various kinds of living creatures marching in three single files in the order in which they are related to have left the Ark: 'both birds, and beasts, and every creeping thing that creepeth upon the earth', *Gen.*

8: 17. In the surviving parts of the border surrounding this panel, beasts of prey are seen pursuing herbivorous animals; and at one spot a blessing upon the Holy Place and the Congregation is inscribed in Greek above and on both sides of a seven-branched candlestick, a ram's horn, a lectern, and a palm-branch. Of the rest of the mosaic, only small fragments remain, including an Aramaic inscription; for the latter see below (p. 77).

4. Synagogues in Greek Lands.

Wherever there were Jews in antiquity, there were naturally synagogues as well, and inscriptions testifying to their existence have been found in abundance throughout the ancient civilized world. Architectural remains from which some idea of the actual structure of these edifices can be obtained, however, are hardly known outside of what used to be the Hellenistic world.

(a) Delos.

The most ancient of these is the synagogue excavated by the École Française d'Athènes on the island of Delos,[1] the smallest member of the group known as the Cyclades, in the Southern Aegean. In virtue of its central position, in the middle of this sea, Delos developed into a very important commercial centre in the centuries immediately preceding the Christian Era. Jews as well as other Oriental merchants were attracted to it; and the Jewish community of the island is mentioned already in Macc. 1:15, 23 (i.e. in the second pre-Christian century), while Josephus (Ant. x: 8, 14) has preserved two official documents referring to it from the first pre-Christian century.

The synagogue is situated at the north-east corner of the island, to the east of the Stadion and at a short distance from the shore (Fig. 10). The building as excavated is divided

[1] A. Plassart, Mélanges Holleaux, recueil de mémoires concernant l'antiquité grecque, Paris, 1913, pp. 201 ff.; also RB, 1914, pp. 523 ff.

into an eastern and a western section. The eastern is almost completely destroyed; what remains of it only suffices to show that along it ran a portico covered at least partially by a roof of tiles, of which many fragments were found during the excavations. Of the western section, embracing the synagogue proper and adjacent rooms, the northern half (Pl. X) consists of two oblong chambers separated by a wall cut through by three doorways. In the opinion of the excavators, this dividing wall is of later date than the rest of the structure, so that it would seem that the two chambers originally constituted one large hall. The more northerly of the present two chambers contains, ranged along the entire length of its western wall, a row of marble benches, from the midst of which stands out the *kathedra* of white marble of which we shall have occasion to speak again (*v.* p. 61).

The character of the edifice is attested by several *ex voto* inscriptions, all in the Greek language, on marble columns and bases. The Deity is always referred to in them as Θεὸς Ὕψιστος[1] (God, the Most High) or just Ὕψιστος (the Most High). This, and the fact that it is situated outside the town and by the water (*v.* p. 49 f.), together with the presence of the word προσευχή in one of the inscriptions—where it seems, in typically Jewish fashion, to be employed as a designation of the institution—renders its Jewish character almost certain.[2]

---

[1] Two inscriptions of Rheneia (Modern Megale Delos), an island only about a kilometre west of Delos and containing its necropolis, invoke in identical terms the vengeance of the Most High God, ὁ Θεὸς ὁ Ὕψιστος, upon the murderers of two women, Marthine and Heraklea. Here this Jewish designation of the Deity is accompanied by references to his angels, ἄγγελοι; and the inscriptions further declare that 'this day every soul is humbled', πᾶσα ψυχὴ ταπεινοῦται.

These epitaphs, which can only have been written by Jews, demonstrate that the same is true of the Θεὸς Ὕψιστος inscriptions of Delos.

[2] *v.* the discussion by Plassart, op. cit.; E. Schürer, *Geschichte des jüdischen Volkes*, ii, p. 500, n.d.

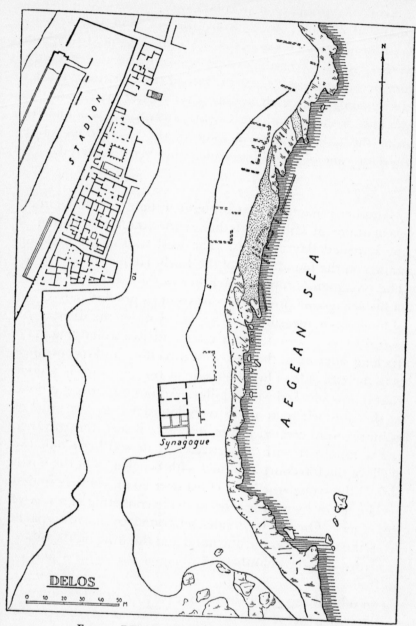

FIG. 10. DELOS, STADION AND SYNAGOGUE.

From the presence in the late wall mentioned above of pieces of marble blocks from the ruins of the near-by Gymnasium, which was destroyed in the War of Mithridates in the year 88 B.C.E., the excavators were able to deduce the late first century B.C.E. as the date of this partition; but for the synagogue as such a somewhat earlier date—possibly the end of the second pre-Christian century—was inferred from the palaeography of some of the inscriptions. It is therefore one of the oldest synagogues yet discovered.

(b) *Miletus.*

Another synagogue was brought to light by the German excavations at Miletus.[1] It lies at the south-west corner of the so-called Bay of Lions. The west wall of the building stands on the foundations of the Early Hellenistic city wall. The synagogue proper, which lies in the south-west corner of the synagogue precincts, consists in its present state of an oblong room, measuring 18·51 m. by 11·60 m., divided by two rows of columns into a nave and two aisles (Fig. 11). Its long sides lie in the east-west direction, and its entrance is in the east side. On either side of this entrance is a door that is now blocked with a pillar. Apparently this was done at the time when, at a relatively late date, the two rows of columns were erected in the interior. Before the entrance lies a forecourt with a peristyle; in its southern half the walls of the forecourt are lined with benches. On the north side of the synagogue lies a court over 20 m. wide, bounded on the north by a wing 6·60 m. wide consisting of a row of chambers. On the west side, separated by narrow spaces from the basilica on the one hand and the wing on the other, is a row of three chambers of unequal size, with a portico in front.

An official record of the early existence of a Jewish community at Miletus has been preserved, as in the case of

---

[1] A. von Gerkan, *ZNW*, 1921, p. 177 f.; id., in *Milet, Ergebnisse u. Untersuchungen seit dem Jahre 1899* (hrsg. von Th. Wiegand), Bd. i, Heft 6: *Der Nordmarkt u. d. Hafen a. d. Löwenbucht*, Berlin-Leipzig, 1922, pp. 80 ff.

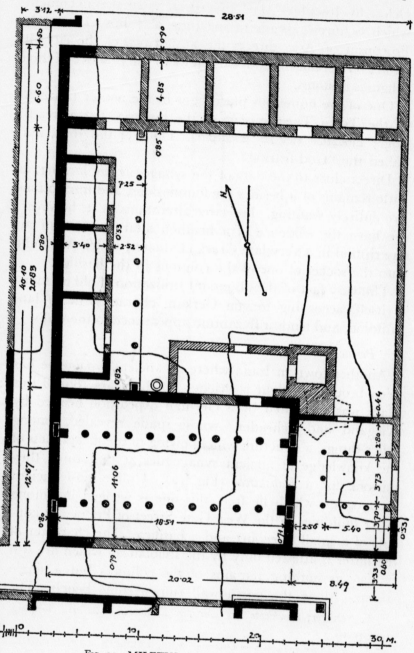

FIG. 11. MILETUS, PLAN OF SYNAGOGUE.

G

Delos, by Josephus (*Ant.* xiv: 10, 21). In this document, which Schürer[1] assigns to the time of Julius Caesar, the Proconsul of Asia directs the authorities of the city, in strong terms, not to hinder the Jews in the practice of their religious customs.

One of the numerous place-signs in the nether Diazoma of the Town Theatre, east of the imperial lodge, reads: Τόπος Εἰουλέων τῶν καὶ Θεοσεβίον, 'Place of the Jews, also called the "God-fearing" '.[2]

Direct clues to the date of the synagogue are lacking, as little remains of it besides the foundations, and inscriptions are entirely wanting. For later alterations in it, however, we have the evidence of a heathen altar stone, with an inscription in a very late Greek character, which was built into the socket of one of the columns in the basilica.

The very fact of the abundant utilization of old masonry is itself, according to von Gerkan, characteristic of late building, and lends a Byzantine appearance to the walls.

(c) *Priene.*

Another town in Ionia where an ancient synagogue has been brought to light is Priene. In the years 1895–8 this place was excavated by a German expedition headed by Wiegand and Schrader,[3] whose spade revealed, among other things, a structure which, owing to the meagreness of the knowledge of ancient synagogues at that time, they mistook for a *Hauskirche* (Fig. 12). Unlike most ancient synagogues, which lie free, this one is wedged in among other buildings in the West Gate Street of Priene. It consists of a small forecourt and a basilica. The character of the latter is attested only by the stylobates—which are still *in situ*—as nothing remains of the columns but a single stump. Along the north wall runs a stone bench. The

[1] E. Schürer, *Geschichte des jüdischen Volkes*, iii, 4th ed., Leipzig, 1909, p. 16.

[2] A. Deissmann, *Licht vom Osten*, 4. Aufl., Tübingen, 1923, p. 391 f.

[3] Th. Wiegand u. M. Schrader, *Priene, Ergebnisse der Ausgrabungen,* Berlin, 1904, p. 480.

excavators were puzzled by the niche in the east wall, 'in
which there was only room for one priest'; by this time we
have learned to recognize it as the repository of the Ark of
the Law.

It will be seen then, that the structure has all the features
of an ancient synagogue. It consists of a forecourt and a

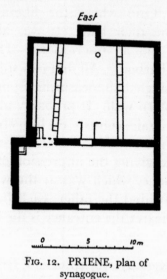

FIG. 12. PRIENE, plan of
synagogue.

basilica, it has benches along the walls, and it has an ark-
niche oriented towards Jerusalem. The matter is clinched
by the blurred traces of a seven-branched candlestick
engraved in a pillar not far from the niche and by another
candlestick, flanked by a bird on either side, on another stone
found in the interior.[1] Certainly derived from this building
is still a third representation of this motive in relief on
a stone that was found built into a church unearthed in the
same excavations.[2] In this relief, now kept in the Kaiser-
Friedrich-Museum, Berlin (Inv. No. 4691), the Menorah is
flanked by a citrus (*Ethrog*) on the one hand and a palm-
branch (*Lulab*) and a ram's horn (*Shofar*) on the other; and
on either side of its shaft, between the branches and the base,
lies a rolled-up scroll of the Law.

[1] Ibid. Fig. 586.   [2] Ibid. Fig. 582.

(d) *Aegina.*

One of the first synagogues to be discovered in Greek lands, and one of which the mosaic floor has also been preserved, is that of Aegina, a well-known little island off Piraeus. Attention was first called to these remains by Ludwig Ross, a scholar attached to the court of the Bavarian Prince Otto whom the liberated Greeks had invited to become their king. It was also he who first copied the two mosaic inscriptions. The synagogue is situated near the harbour. All that can still be traced of its architecture is a single hall measuring 13 m. by 7·60 m. and an apse in its eastern wall. It probably also had a portico in front. The mosaic consists exclusively of geometrical designs in blue, grey, red, and black, tastefully combined and executed, and giving the impression of a carpet.

Near the entrance, which was at the west end, are two inscriptions one behind the other, each framed in a *tabula ansata.* The one nearer the entrance is the larger, consisting of three lines:

1. Θεόδωρος ἀρ[χισυνάγωγος φρ]οντίσας ἔτη τέσσερα
2. ἐχ θεμελίων τὴν σ[υναγωγὴν] οἰκοδόμησα προσοδεύθησαν
3. χρύσινοι ʹπεʹ καὶ ἐκ τῶν τοῦ θεοῦ Δωρεῶν χρύσινοι ʹρεʹ

1. I, Theodoros, the Archisynagogos, who functioned for four years,
2. built this synagogue from its foundations. Revenues amounted to
3. 85 pieces of gold (i.e. gold dinars), and offerings unto God to 105 pieces of gold.

The second inscription has apparently suffered further damage since it was first discovered. The early reading of it as well as its present state yield the sense that the mosaic was paved during the term of office of Theodoros the younger or, according to another reading, the νεωκόρος (an honorary title). The concluding formula is apparently to be restored: [εὐλ]ογία πᾶσιν το[ῖς παρεσχημέ]νοις, 'Blessing be upon all the donors'. Compare the similar benedictions from Palestinian synagogue mosaics quoted below (pp. 73 ff.).

This mosaic floor was exposed again and copied by Dr. G. Welter and the writer in 1928, Pl. XI being one of the fruits of these operations. The recent completion of the excavation of this site[1] revealed the fact that the Theodoros synagogue was built over an older one with the same orientation and lay-out. It apparently remained standing until the seventh century, and the materials of which it was constructed were subsequently for the most part utilized in new buildings.

[1] *Jahrbuch d. Archäolog. Instituts d. Deutschen Reichs*, 1932, Archäologischer Anzeiger, pp. 164 f.

CHAPTER III

1. *Architecture of the Synagogues.*

ALL the ancient synagogues that have thus far come to light in Palestine are built in the form of a basilica with a nave and two aisles. It goes without saying, however, that this style of architecture was introduced under Hellenistic influence, and it may be assumed that the main hall of a synagogue building was not originally divided into aisles. Archaeological evidence for this has thus far, it is true, not been found in Palestine itself, but this is no doubt due to the fact that the oldest architectural remains of synagogues which are still extant do not go back farther than the third century C.E. We have seen that the synagogues of Delos (second century C.E.), Aegina (built on the foundations of, and on the same plan as, an older one), and Miletus, were all, at least originally, built without the dividing columns (*v.* pp. 37 ff.). In time the basilica, which was so universally employed in the Hellenistic world for public buildings of various sorts, became the standard type of building for Jewish synagogues as well, which were not merely places of worship but also of study and public instruction in the Law, of communal assemblies, &c. An early application of the basilica style of Jewish public institutions in Palestine is exemplified by the Chamber of Hewn Stone, לשכת הגזית (*b. Yoma* 15 a), in which the Jewish Supreme Court held its sittings; but we know also (*Mishna, Tamid*, 4: 3 end) that this hall served as a synagogue.[1] Of Jewish basilicas outside of Palestine, the most famous is the 'Diplostoon of Alexandria', which was also used as a synagogue (*Tosephta, Sukkah* 4: 6, *j. Sukkah* 55 a–b; *b. Sukkah* 51 b).

The Talmuds, which in general have preserved very few details about the architecture of synagogues, nevertheless refer frequently to one of its features, namely the columns (e.g. *j. Berakhot* 12 a; *b.* ibid. 27 b).

[1] Cf. S. Krauss, *Synagogale Altertümer*, Berlin-Wien, 1922, p. 68 n.

The three entrances, which are a feature of the majority of Palestine synagogues, have also left a trace of themselves in literature ('the middle portal of the Beth Midrash', *j. Berakhot* 11 c bottom; 'the middle portal of the old synagogue of Tiberias', *Leviticus Rabba* xxii).

The benches for the congregation lined the walls, and when they did not suffice, some no doubt sat on mats on the floor.

The ancient literature nowhere mentions a specific regulation to the effect that the men and women must be kept separate at public worship; still less is it prescribed that the women's section shall be built in the form of a gallery. That the sexes were in fact kept apart in synagogues, however, is already attested by Philo (*apud* Eusebius, *Praep. Evang.* 8: 12),[1] the custom having probably been taken over by the synagogue from the Jerusalem Sanctuary. For, as regards the Herodian Temple, we have numerous references to 'the Women's Forecourt' (עזרת הנשים) as distinct from 'the People's Forecourt' (עזרת ישראל), the latter being the more inner one. The Water-Drawing Celebration, however, which took place on the night following upon the first day of the Feast of Tabernacles, was held in the Women's Forecourt, and thus a further regulation became necessary. The Babylonian Talmud relates (*Sukkah*, 51 b bottom): 'At first the women used to be within and the men without, and frivolity would result; accordingly it was ordained that the women should sit without and the men within, but still there was frivolity. Finally it was ordained that the women should sit above and the men below.' As it was only on this one occasion that men occupied the women's forecourt, the Talmud is no doubt right in connecting this Baraitha with the *Mishna Middoth* 2: 5: 'It (the Women's Forecourt) was at first even, but later it was surrounded with a gallery (כצוצטרה ἐξώστρα), so that the women looked on from above and the men from below, in order that they should not be together.'

There is therefore every reason to suppose that the

[1] Cf. J. Juster, *Les Juifs dans l'Empire romain*, Paris, 1914, i, p. 458 n.

galleries of which remains have been found in several of the ancient synagogues of Palestine served, as in modern synagogues, as a women's section.[1] The gallery ran along three walls of the basilica. Along the two long walls it was supported by the two rows of columns of the basilica, and these were frequently joined by a third at the end nearest the short wall that was occupied by the gallery. In the case of Beth Alpha, where such a connecting row of columns is absent, the short section of the gallery was built over the portico and supported by the columns of the latter. The staircases leading up to the gallery are always situated outside the basilica proper, leaning against either the outer or inner walls of one of the annexed chambers.

The functions of the annexes may be taken with some certainty to have been those of class-rooms for children and

[1] Dr. H. L. Ginsberg kindly calls my attention to a piece of literary evidence for the existence and function of the gallery, which M. Ish-Shalom (Friedmann), *Beth Talmud* v: 200 f., was the first to detect.

According to *j. Sukkah* 55 b, the Diplostoon (*v.* p. 46) was destroyed in the Jewish Rebellion in the reign of the Emperor Trajan. The latter is there related to have come upon the Jews just at the moment when they were 'dealing with' the verse *Dt.* 28: 48; that is to say, either during 'the Reading of the Law' or during a sermon. That the scene is the Diplostoon is evident enough from the Palestinian Talmud itself, but is explicitly stated in the brief parallel notice *b.* ibid. 51 b bottom; and the editor of the Proem to *Esther Rabba*, who cites the passage in an abridged form, at least makes it refer to Egypt. After killing the men, Trajan offers mercy to the women at the price of their honour, but they reply, 'Do to those above (עילייא) as you have done to those below (ארעייא)'. Right or wrong, the Palestinian narrator cannot conceive of the Community Centre in Alexandria otherwise than with a gallery, and that reserved for the women.

Accordingly it would seem that the reading of the parallels in the ordinary edition of *Lamentations Rabba*, 58 b and 68 d, where the terms are reversed, is due to a misapprehension. In Buber's edition, p. 83, they are simply replaced by 'men' and 'women'.

It is even possible that in Palestinian Aramaic the male and female halves of any congregation were designated colloquially as ארעייא, literally 'those of the ground (floor)' and עילייא, 'those of the upper (floor)' respectively.

guest-rooms for strangers. That strangers frequently lodged in synagogues is attested by several passages in the Talmud; and the inscription of the synagogue of Theodotos in Jerusalem (*v.* p. 69 f.) makes special mention of the guest-house. The performance of each of the ceremonies of the sanctification of the Sabbath and Festivals (*Qiddush*) and the ushering in of the week-days (*Habdala*) first in the synagogue and then, almost immediately afterwards, in the home—which now looks like useless repetition—had its origin in the fact that very often some of the congregants had no home to go to after the services but remained to eat their evening meal and spend the night in the synagogue.[1]

A courtyard, which might be situated on any side of the synagogue, contained vessels with water for the washing of the hands before prayer.

2. *Situation of the Synagogues.*

Regarding the situation of synagogues, the Talmudical canon prescribes only one regulation, namely that they shall be built on the highest sites in the towns. The Palestinian synagogues mostly satisfy this specification. That it was not always observed in Babylon is evident from the manner in which it is urged by the religious authorities of that country (*b. Shabbath* 11 a). It may have become impolitic there as it did later in the Diaspora generally, and even in Palestine. To Christian populations, at any rate, the presence of synagogues everywhere in the most prominent spots in the cities was provoking.

Although official Judaism has preserved no trace of a precept to that effect, there is abundant evidence that Jews in Hellenistic countries built their synagogues by preference in the proximity of water. Josephus, *Ant.* xiv. 10, 23, para. 258, tells of a decision of the people of Halicarnassus to suffer the Jews to observe their laws and sabbaths and build synagogues, as was their custom, by the sea. At Philippi, the apostle Paul and his companions went forth on

[1] Cf. the benediction, p. 74 n. 1.

H

a Sabbath outside the town gate near the river, where they
supposed there was a synagogue (*Acts* 14: 13).[1]

As we have seen, the synagogues of Delos, Aegina, and
Miletus in fact lie close to the edge of the shore. There is
not sufficient archaeological evidence for the existence of
such a tradition in Palestine, though it is true that the
synagogue of Capernaum is situated outside the ancient
town and close to the Sea of Galilee.

3. *Orientation of the Synagogues.*

Ancient synagogues in Palestine were built facing
Jerusalem. Of course the direction was only approximate;
for some concession had to be made to the lay of the ground,
and even apart from that absolute accuracy does not seem
to have been aimed at.

Thus the majority of ancient Palestinian synagogues,
being situated in Cisjordania north of Jerusalem, are
appropriately oriented to the south, though with variations
of several degrees, but those in Transjordania, even as far
north as the Sea of Galilee, face west. At Semmaka, a village
on Mt. Carmel, the proximity of the Mediterranean, which
forms the western boundary of Palestine, seems to have been
the factor that determined the orientation of the ruined
synagogue found there to the east instead of to the south.
No ancient synagogues have been found south of Jerusalem,
but presumably they faced north.

As regards synagogues outside Palestine, it may be
assumed *a priori*, pending the emergence of archaeological

[1] It seems plausible to seek the motive for this Jewish custom of the
Diaspora in טומאת ארץ העמים, the ritual uncleanness of the land of
the Gentiles, in view of the following passage from the Midrash: 'And
although, for the Merit of the Fathers, He spoke unto them (the
Prophets) outside the Land, yet did He only speak unto them in a
clean place, by water: as it is written, "and I was by the stream Ulai"
(Dn. 8: 2); "as I was by the great river, which is Tigris" (Dn. 10: 4);
and as it is further written, "the word of the Lord come expressly, etc.,
in the land of the Chaldaeans by the river Chebar" (Ezek. 1: 3).'—
Mekhilta to Ex. 12: 1.

evidence, that other countries east of Palestine followed the same practice as Transjordania. It is certain that in the regions to the west of Palestine the synagogues were oriented to the east. Such is the case at Miletus, Priene, Aegina, and elsewhere. For Egypt we have the following testimony of Apion,[1] who was of course merely attributing to Moses a contemporary Jewish practice with which he was familiar:

'Moses, as I have heard from old people in Egypt, was a native of Heliopolis, who, being pledged to the customs of his country, erected prayer-houses, open to the air, in the various precincts of the city, all facing eastwards; such being the orientation also of Heliopolis . . .'

The practice of orientation in prayer certainly dates from the Biblical period. The famous Prayer of Solomon upon the dedication of the Temple built by him contains the following passage (1 K. 8: 44): 'If Thy people go out to battle against their enemy, by whatsoever way Thou shalt send them, and they pray unto the Lord toward the city which Thou hast chosen, and toward the house which I have built for Thy name; then hear Thou in heaven their prayer and their supplication, and maintain their cause.' The case of war-captives is also contemplated, and it is craved that (ibid. 48 f.) 'if they return unto Thee with all their heart and with all their soul in the land of their enemies, who carried them captive, and pray unto Thee toward their land, which Thou gavest unto their fathers, the city which Thou hast chosen, and the house which I have built for Thy name; then hear Thou their prayer and their supplication . . .' (and similarly in 2 Chr. 6: 34 ff.)

Of Daniel it is related that (Dn. 6: 11) 'he went into his house—now his windows were open in his upper chamber towards Jerusalem—and he kneeled upon his knees three times a day, and prayed . . .'

Of post-Biblical literature, the Tosephta, Berakhoth, ch. 3,

[1] Josephus, Contra Apionem, ii. 10.

prescribes as follows: 'Those standing outside the Land of Israel shall direct their hearts towards the Land of Israel and pray, for it is written, "and pray unto the Lord toward their Land, &c."[1] Those standing in the Land of Israel shall direct their hearts unto Jerusalem and pray, for it is written, "and they shall pray towards this city".[1] Those standing in Jerusalem shall direct their hearts towards the Sanctuary and pray, for it is written, "and they shall pray towards this Place".[1] Thus, those standing in the north face to the south; those standing in the south face to the north; those standing in the east face to the west; those standing in the west face to the east; so that all Israel direct their prayers towards one spot.'

Although these rules are intended for individual worshippers, the orientation of the houses of worship was determined by them.

4. *Interior Equipment of the Synagogues.*

The Ark of the Law. In the Rabbinical sources of the early centuries of the current era, the Ark of the Law is often spoken of not as a stationary object but as a portable chest containing the scrolls of the Law, which was no doubt kept in a closet or small chamber and carried into the main hall of the synagogue for the services.[2] The archaeological finds confirm this. We have already seen (p. 19) that the Ark of the Capernaum synagogue was constructed in such a way as to render the elaborate main portal useless. It was evidently an afterthought. As the synagogue came to occupy a more and more central position in Jewish religious life, there was a tendency to increase its impressiveness by the permanent presence of the most sacred ritual object, the Scroll of the Law; for which later a special repository in the form of an apse was constructed. In the older synagogues, like those of Capernaum or Chorazin,

---

[1] The quotations in the *Tosephta* agree with the text of 2 *Chr.* 6: 34 ff., the parallel version of Solomon's prayer.

[2] *Mishna, Ta'anith* 2: 1; *Tosephta, Megilla* 4: 21; *b. Sotah* 39 b.

a special stone structure, of which some remains have been preserved, was secondarily erected just inside the main entrance, thus blocking it. Presumably the same thing happened in other places at about the same period, and the absence of any such remains there may be due to the arks having as a rule been made of wood as in modern times.

Scanty, however, as are the actual remains of Arks of the Law, we can get a good idea of their structure and appearance from quite a number of contemporary pictorial representations of them that have come down to us both from Palestine and the Diaspora. These illustrations agree remarkably among themselves as regards all the main features, which can hardly be accounted for otherwise than by the fact that the type of Ark actually used in the synagogues was pretty uniform everywhere. It is a sort of double-doored chest with a gabled or rounded roof. Each of the door-wings was divided horizontally into a number of square or oblong panels. The door-posts were sometimes shaped like columns. The pediment was also ornamented, sometimes with a shell in the centre (Fig. 13).

A view of the interior of the Ark is offered by the Jewish gilt glass vessels found in the catacombs of Rome (Fig. 14). Here the Ark is as a rule represented with open doors, showing the scrolls, each rolled about a rod (umbilicus, ὀμφαλός, עמוד) lying in rows on shelves. In one of these pictures we see on the shelves instead of scrolls the cases in which they were kept. The scroll-case, הספר (θήκη) תיק, is familiar to students of the Rabbinical literature.

The Lectern. Another object connected with the scroll of the Law is the Lectern (Heb. אנלוגין *Tosephta, Kelim* 5: 6, 9, from Gr. ἀναλογεῖον). In antiquity this was a comparatively light object, rather like our music-stands, and could even be hung up when not in use.[1] Of this too, apparently, pictorial representations survive in the mosaic floor of the

[1] Th. Birt, *Die Buchrolle in der Kunst*, Leipzig, 1907, pp. 157 ff., especially Fig. 113.

FIG. 13. PEQI'IN, figure of Ark.
(By permission of the Palestine Exploration Fund.)

FIG. 14. JEWISH GILT GLASS.

synagogues at Beth Alpha and Jerash, on lamps (Fig. 15), in a relief on a capital at Capernaum, &c.[1]

The Seven-branched Candlestick. The pictorial representations of synagogue appurtenances include the seven-branched candlestick or Menorah. The view that the intention of such pictures is to represent not a picture of contemporary houses of worship but the candlestick of the Temple is untenable, though it has many advocates. It is true that the Menorah was regarded as a sort of sacred emblem, no doubt because of its association with the Tabernacle of the Testimony and the Jerusalem Sanctuary, but the stone candlestick found at Tiberias shows that it was at the same time an object in actual use

FIG. 15. Lamp with figures of synagogual appurtenances.

in synagogues of the early centuries of the Christian Era. The stone candlestick just mentioned was discovered in the ancient synagogue of Ḥammath-by-Tiberias, חמתא דטבריה, which was excavated by N. Slouschz in 1921 on behalf of the Jewish Palestine Exploration Society (Pl. XII *a*). It is cut out of a single block of limestone and measures 60 cm. in width by 46 cm. in height, and 13 cm. in thickness. On the face side of the branches are carved pomegranates alternating with flowers. No spaces are carved out between the upper ends of the branches, so that the top of the candlestick consists of one continuous slab. In the upper surface of this, seven grooves are hollowed out, corresponding to the seven branches and destined to contain seven earthen lamps.

The pictures of synagogue appurtenances sometimes contain only one candlestick and sometimes two. Cases of the latter, however, do not prove that there were two candle-

[1] For my former interpretation of these pictures as further representations of Torah-cases with rods, see *The Ancient Synagogue of Beth Alpha*, pp. 27 ff.

sticks in the synagogue; for they may merely be due to a desire for symmetry, as such pictures are also otherwise symmetrical about their vertical axes. At any rate, as we have seen, only one Menorah was found by the excavators at Ḥammath.

The realism of the artistry on the glass vessels from the

FIG. 16. JEWISH GILT GLASS.

catacombs of Rome (Fig. 16) and on the mosaics of synagogue floors in Palestine is further illustrated by the lions which are there represented as flanking the Ark. The trunks or fragments of such lions found in the synagogue ruins of Capernaum, Chorazin, and Kafr Bir'im have already been mentioned (Pl. XIII).

The Veil. The pictorial representations of which we have been speaking have also preserved for us some notion of the veil, פרוכת, by which the recess containing the Ark was divided off from the rest of the hall. They show us that it was hung not, as in modern times, over the doors of the Ark, but in front of the whole apse.

In the Beth Alpha synagogue the floor of the apse is

raised and projects into the main hall for some distance as a platform cut through in the middle by stairs. On the edge of this platform, on either side of the stairs, is a socket. The sockets no doubt contained two posts, supporting a bar or wire from which the veil hung down. We can see two such posts in front of the Ark in a decoration on one of the gilded glass vessels first published by De Rossi, who believed, like many after him, that they symbolized the Jachin and Boaz of the Solomonic Temple; but it is now certain that the artist was merely faithfully copying from contemporary Arks.[1]

The Screen. Another means of separating the recess of the Ark from the worshippers was a marble screen, like the iconostasis of Christian churches. Remains of such screens, sometimes decorated with wreaths, Menorahs, vines, &c., have come to light in several places (Ḥammath (Pl. XII *b*), Ascalon (Pl. XIV), Ashdod, and elsewhere).

The Bema. The spot where the lesson of the week was recited was raised above the rest of the floor. This platform, βῆμα, בימה, which is present in every larger synagogue to-day, is frequently mentioned in the Talmudic literature. Apparently it was usually constructed of wood, and therefore perished under the unfavourable climatic conditions of Palestine. An actual bema—this time in stone—has been found only in one place in Palestine, Beth Alpha, near the second pillar from the south of the eastern row, not far from the apse. That it is of later date than the mosaic is evident from the fact that it stands on it. It was probably built near the end of the sixth century. There is a more elaborate structure, hewn out of basalt in the al-Ḥayyât Mosque of Aleppo (Fig. 17); this mosque was formerly a synagogue, and still contains a Hebrew inscription, and has been shown by Herzfeld and Sobernheim to date from the sixth century.[2]

The Seat of Moses. The excavations of recent years have brought to light a feature of ancient synagogues, the famous reference to which in the New Testament ('in the Seat of

---

[1] For a discussion of this question see my *Beth Alpha*, pp. 19 ff.
[2] *Festschrift Sachan*, Berlin, 1915, pp. 311 ff.

Moses', *Matt.* 23: 2) used formerly to be interpreted in a
purely symbolical way. The first 'Seat of Moses' was
unearthed at Ḥammath-by-Tiberias, and was followed by

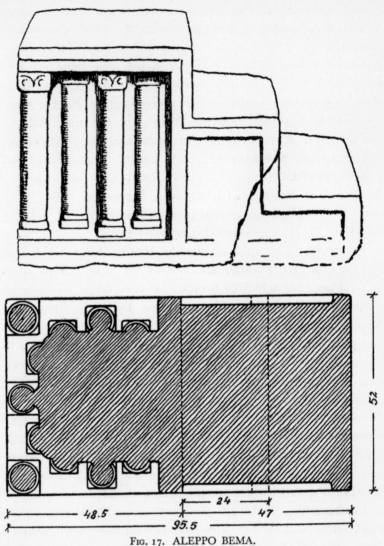

FIG. 17. ALEPPO BEMA.

another at Chorazin. We know that whereas the congregation sat on the stone benches that are still found along the
side walls of many of the ancient synagogues, or else on
mats on the floor, 'the elders' sat 'with their faces to the

people and their backs to the Holy (i.e. to Jerusalem)',
Tosephta, Megilla 4: 21. It was evidently for the most distinguished among 'the elders' that the stone chair found
near the south wall of the Ḥammath synagogue was reserved.
This was no doubt 'the Seat of Moses'. That 'the καθέΔρα

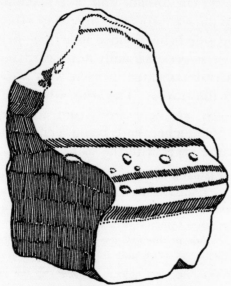

FIG. 18. ḤAMMATH-BY-TIBERIAS
Seat of Moses.

of Moses' was a familiar physical object and not an abstrac-
tion is proved by the fact that a Palestinian scholar of the
fourth century could facilitate the understanding of the
Biblical description of Solomon's throne ('and the top of the
throne was round behind', 1 *K.* 10: 19) for his audience by
the simple explanation כהדא קתדרא דמשה 'like the καθέΔρα of
Moses' (*Pesiqta de Rab Kahana*, ed. Buber, p. 12).[1]

The *kathedra* found at Ḥammath-by-Tiberias[2] is rather
crudely carved out of a single block of white limestone
(Fig. 18). Its rounded top is partly damaged. It is 94 cm.
high and 60 cm. broad. As stated, this *kathedra* was found
in situ next to the wall orientated towards Jerusalem.

[1] W. Bacher, 'Le siège de Moïse', *REJ*, xxxiv (1897), pp. 299 ff.
[2] For the literature see *Tarbiz*, 1–A, pp. 145 ff.

Much more finished is the execution of the *kathedra* found at Chorazin.[1] Like the rest of the synagogue it is of basalt, and like its homologue in Ḥammath it is carved out of one block (Pl. XV). The *kathedra* is in a fair state of preservation, though small parts are missing here and there. It is 56 cm. high, 73 cm. broad, and of a maximum thickness of 56·5 cm. in the seat proper. Three of its sides are straight, only the front side being divided into three fields, of which the middle one slopes diagonally downward and backward. The support is ornamented in front with a rosette, as can be seen in the illustration. The arms, which are of one piece with the body, are separated from it except at their extremities, the higher end being continuous with the support and the lower with the seat.[2]

[1] Though not found *in situ*, it too doubtless originally stood next to the south wall, for it was found not far from it, and would seem to have been hurled down, together with other architectural features on this side of the house, in a rather violent earthquake.

[2] On the front side of this *kathedra* is engraved the following much-discussed inscription (as I am now inclined to read and interpret it):

(1) דכיר לטב יודן בר ישמעל (2) דעבד הדן סטוה (3) ודרגוה בפעלה יהי
(4) לה חולק עם צדיקים

1. Remembered be for good Judan b. Ishmael 2. who made this στοά 3. and its staircase. As his reward may 4. he have a share with the righteous.

In reading בפעלה (l. 3), I have adopted the suggestion of J. N. Epstein (*Tarbiz*, I, c, p. 152). I cannot, however, agree with him in making סטוה refer to the *kathedra* on which the inscription is engraved. Whilst it is true that the Aramaic סטוה, spelt in various ways, very often designates a low bench or counter, usually one projecting from a wall or fixed to the floor, it is never used of a chair for a single person. In our inscription סטוה no doubt has the ordinary meaning of στοά, viz. 'colonnade', and refers to the whole synagogue. For as we have seen, it is built like a basilica, and its interior is divided into three aisles by two rows of columns. We have also seen that it is built on raised ground and approached by two well-built staircases; so that the reference in the inscription to the 'steps' of the στοά is understandable if the latter means the synagogue, but meaningless if it is the *kathedra*.

A. Marmorstein (*PEF. Q. St.* 1927, p. 101 f.) admits the possibility of Judan b. Ishmael being identical with Judan b. Ishmael, the Scribe,

Perhaps closer to the period of the New Testament is the handsome marble seat (Fig. 19) found in the ruins of the synagogue at Delos.[1] It is still *in situ*, and rather surprisingly faces east; but the elders need not have sat, as was customary

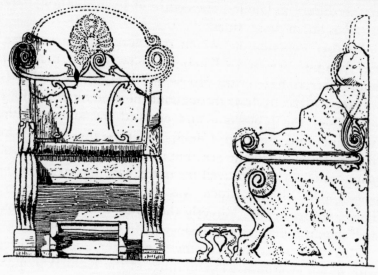

FIG. 19. DELOS, SEAT OF MOSES.

but not necessarily obligatory in Palestine, 'with their backs to the Holy'.

5. *Ornamentation of the Synagogues.*

A phenomenon which was the cause of much wonderment among scholars at the time when ancient synagogues first began to be studied and excavated in Palestine—in these days really only in Galilee—was the frequency of pictorial representations of animals and human beings; which Jewish rigorism frowns upon. A theory was evolved that the synagogues found were the work of sections of

a person of the third century who is mentioned in the Rabbinical sources; but the data obviously do not suffice either to prove or to disprove such identity, as Marmorstein himself felt.

[1] Sven Risom, 'Le siège du prêtre de Dionysos' in *Mélanges Holleaux, Recueil de mémoires concernant l'Antiquité grecque*, Paris, 1913, pp. 257 ff.

Galilaean Jewry which took a more liberal view of the matter than the orthodox authorities. It was realized, however, that so widespread a lack of discipline as is indicated by the number of such synagogues was rather extraordinary in Galilee, the centre of Jewish national and religious life in those times.[1]

Another explanation, which still has adherents to-day, was then put forward by Kitchener; namely that, inasmuch as the Patriarchate of the House of Hillel, whose authority was recognized by Jews throughout the Roman dominions, was under the protection and enjoyed the favour of the Antonine and Severan Caesars, it was the latter who 'inspired and aided the erection of these synagogues', and, being ignorant though well meaning, thus forced upon the worshippers an art which was contumely in their sight. These, consequently, 'directly they were able . . . deserted such pagan buildings as a disloyalty to their religion'.[2]

This view was taken up by Watzinger and supported with much erudition. The findings of the Kohl-Watzinger excavations seemed to confirm it, for in all the synagogues there was unmistakable evidence of iconoclasm and of its having been perpetrated at a time when they were still in use. Watzinger therefore concluded that the elders of the Jews had no choice but to accept the gifts whose richness proclaims their imperial source, even if some of the features in them offended their religious feelings, but took advantage of the extinction of the Severan dynasty to destroy the prohibited images.

Tempting as this hypothesis is, however, it must yield before the eloquent silence of both the literary sources and the comparatively numerous inscriptions found in the synagogues themselves. How could the memory of such munificent donations, whose bestowal would have been an act of great political significance, and the memory of which

[1] Kohl and Watzinger, op. cit., p. 202 f.

[2] H. H. Kitchener, ' Synagogues of Galilee', *PEF. Q. St.* 1878, pp. 123 ff.

could not have died while the synagogues in question were still standing and in daily use, have failed to leave any trace in Jewish literature? The Palestinian Talmud has preserved an account of the donation of a candelabrum to a synagogue, by a non-Jew (Antoninus), *j. Megilla* 74 a, but nowhere is there any allusion to endowments on such a large scale as that assumed by this theory.

But the whole conception of the Jewish attitude towards pictorial representations of living beings which gave rise to such theories needs to be revised. The letter of *Ex.* 20: 4; *Dt.* 5: 8 admits formally of being constructed as a prohibition of all such representations, and there has always been a school in Jewry that has so construed it. But clearly the intention of the Lawgiver, whose language is here not juristically precise, was to qualify this verse by the following one, and only to prohibit the worshipping of images or the making of images for purposes of worship; and there has always been a less austere school in Jewry that has so understood it. Those who canonized the account of the ornaments of Solomon's Temple, 1 *K.* 6–7; 2 *Chr.* 3–4, or of his throne, 2 *Chr.* 9—cherubim, bulls, and lions—cannot have found anything in it to offend their religious feelings. Ezekiel's vision of the restored Temple includes the faces of cherubim, lions, and men as decorative motives, *Ezek.* 41: 18–20, and this fact did not stand in the way of the canonization of this book either. The famous Arch of Titus, on which are depicted the spoils of the Herodian Temple, shows us the seven-branched candlestick decorated with sea-horses, &c., in relief. Likenesses of animals, both painted on the walls and in relief, are a feature of orthodox synagogues to this day, notwithstanding they have repeatedly been a cause of controversy.[1] As might be expected, in more normal

---

[1] See the material by L. Löw, *Graphische Requisiten und Erzeugnisse der Juden*, Leipzig, 1870, pp. 35 ff. An incident from modern times is typical of the whole history of such controversies. The interior of the largest and best-known synagogue in Jerusalem is graced by a very obvious illustration of the Rabbinic adage, 'Be fierce as the leopard,

times the latitudinarian tendency prevailed, whilst crises and persecutions provoked particularistic and rigoristic reactions. Often, too, men were glad to find that they would be fulfilling a religious duty by giving vent to racial passions or pursuing the dictates of policy. Thus in the demolition of the eagle over the Temple Gate by the Zealots (Josephus, *Wars*, i. 33: 2–3), the fact that it was the emblem of Rome was the decisive factor, and to the destruction of the hellenistically ornamented palace in Tiberias (*Vita*, xii) the local leaders were incited by Josephus, obviously with the object of bringing his rival Justus into disfavour with its owner, the Tetrarch Agrippa.

The testimony in this regard of R. Eleazar b. R. Zadok, who had known Jerusalem well before its destruction, is of the highest significance: 'In Jerusalem there were faces of all creatures except men' (*Tosephta*, '*Aboda Zara* 5 (6): 2.[1] This statement is immediately preceded by another of R. Hananiah the son of the Patriarch Gamaliel to the effect that 'Our family used to employ a seal with faces engraved on it'. Further sanctions of this nature are cited in *Tosephta*, '*Aboda Zara*, l.c.; *b.* '*Aboda Zara*, 42 c, *j.* '*Aboda Zara*, 42 b–32 a, and evidently they were all exceeded in real life.

The only rational explanation of the situation found in the ancient synagogues is therefore that pictorial art had its ups and downs in Jewish history, a period of greater laxity being followed by a reaction; and the synagogues of Palestine afford us a peculiarly valuable evidence of both the latitude that at one time prevailed in that country and the later reaction against it.

The Talmudic literature distinguishes degrees of gravity

---

swift as the eagle, fleet as the deer, and brave as the lion to perform the will of thy Father in Heaven', *Mishna Aboth*, 5: 20. At the time when it was painted the Chief Rabbi voiced a protest, but it is still there, and the most pious Jews still worship at this place.

[1] Similarly, 'Eleazar b. R. Zadok' should be read for 'Eleazar b. R. Simeon' in *j.* '*Aboda Zara*, 42 c.

in the offence of iconography, and from it we may imagine, though we cannot prove, that the Palestinian authorities first set their faces against sculptures but still tolerated wall paintings and mosaics; then, with increasing persecution and misery, also vented their bitterness upon two-dimensional representations of animals and human beings. The first phase is attested, for example, by Capernaum, with its mutilated animal reliefs by the side of undamaged vegetable ones, and the second by the floor of 'Ain Dûk, whose Zodiac was deliberately smashed whilst the accompanying inscriptions were spared. As we have seen, synagogues that were abandoned prior to a certain date, such as those of Jerash and Beth Alpha, escaped this fate. Regarding Chorazin, at which most of the figures have been preserved intact, we have an explicit statement by Eusebius and Jerome[1] that it was already uninhabited at the time when they lived in Palestine; and the fourth century may therefore be taken as a *terminus a quo* for the reaction against sculpture. On the other hand, the Beth Alpha mosaic, with its Zodiac and seasons and its picture of the sacrifice of Isaac, was actually paved as late as the sixth century, and the latter date may be taken as the *terminus a quo* for the reaction against this genre of art.

The latter circumstance suggests that a contributing factor in the final banishment of human and animal motives from the synagogues of Palestine may have been the influence of the iconoclastic movement that set in among the Monophysite Christians of the Near East at about this time and which has likewise left its traces in broken church mosaics; the conquest of the country by the Arabs, bearers of a religion unequivocally hostile to the representation of living beings, could of course only have intensified this environmental suggestion.

The motives occurring in synagogue art are included for the most part under the categories of Biblical, astral (zodiac) or magical, and prophylactic (hexagram, penta-

[1] *Onomasticon*, ed. Klostermann, pp. 303, 78 f.

K

gram, Heraclean knot, &c.), motives. Although it cannot
be proved that the latter were consciously employed as
apotropaea, there is a considerable amount of probability
in its favour, for the prevalence even among official Jewish
circles in the Talmudic period of beliefs in evil spirits and
black magic, and in means of frustrating and escaping
their actions, requires no proof for any one at all familiar
with the Rabbinical literature. And Holy Places are
notoriously a particularly attractive target for devils and
sorcerers.

The representations of the Zodiac are also connected with
superstition. The belief in astrology was universal in
ancient times, and is still very widespread to-day, even in
western countries, so that it would have been very extraordinary indeed if the Jews had escaped it. It is true that
from Biblical times (cf. *Jer.* 10: 1 ff.) to the Talmudic Era—
cf. the classical dictum אין מזל לישראל—the doctrine tried to
gain acceptance that Israel, or at least the pious Jew, was
not subject to the influence of the heavenly bodies, but such
influence was not denied in principle. Striking proofs of
the importance attached to 'the constellations' (מזלות) in
the belief of the Jews are Philo's interpretation of the twelve
stones of the High Priest's breastplate (which the Pentateuch
itself declares to be emblems of the twelve tribes of Israel)
as symbols of the twelve signs of the Zodiac; Josephus'
similar explanation (*Wars*, v. 5, 8) of the twelve loaves of
bread in the Tabernacle, and *piyyuṭim* of Kalir and others
which are based on the twelve constellations (*Mazzaloth*).

A cycle of Biblical motives has, it is true, thus far been
found only on mosaics, but from a statement in the Jerusalem Talmud it is evident that mural pictorial art was also
practised by Jews in Palestine, and it is not unlikely that
such will also come to light in synagogues. In those hitherto
excavated, the walls have either been entirely wanting or
else they have lost all their distemper except for a few slight
traces; but these traces are coloured.

As only three synagogue mosaics with Biblical motives

have thus far been recovered (*v.* p. 23 ff.) it is impossible to decide as yet whether they were selected on any particular principle. It is suggestive, however, that Daniel in the Lions' Den, the Sacrifice of Isaac, and the Flood, are all themes that figure in the liturgy. The pictures of Biblical scenes may therefore have been deliberately chosen in order to illustrate and evoke the spirit of the prayers.

A richer cycle of Biblical motives has survived to this day in popular Jewish art, whose origin no doubt go back to antiquity.

All this is no doubt pertinent to the question of the origins of early Christian art. At the beginning of this century Strzygowski, struck by the fact that the frescoes of the early Christian catacombs of Rome employed Old Testament themes exclusively whilst motives from the New Testament only appeared in the later ones, developed a theory which he expounded in a work whose thesis is summed up in its title: *Orient oder Rom?* According to him, the early Church, whose Gospel was preached in Jewish synagogues and professed by men of Jewish race, took over the art of the synagogue along with its liturgy. He accordingly predicted that should any remains of ancient Jewish art come to light again they would confirm his hypothesis. This prediction has been partially fulfilled by the mosaics of the synagogues that have since been unearthed, but it must be added that the question can only be settled when earlier remains are found; for the Palestinian mosaics in question are later than the catacomb frescoes. But at any rate, we are now nearer a solution of this problem.

Regarding the representations of synagogue appurtenances, which also constitute an important cycle, see the discussion of their interpretation in the preceding section.

The geometrical figures and motives from vegetable life, which are partly descended from Jewish coin and ossuary decorations and partly borrowed from contemporary Greco-Roman art, will not receive special treatment here.

6. *Dating of the Synagogues.*

Problems of synagogue dating have already been touched upon here and there in the progress of our discourse. Since dated inscriptions are generally absent,[1] recourse must be had to indirect evidence. As we have seen (p. 3) the Jewish tradition of the Middle Ages ascribed the Galilean synagogues to R. Simeon b. Yoḥai, a scholar of the second century c.e., and the early scientific explorers likewise proposed dates near the turning-point of the second and third centuries. An exhaustive discussion will be found in Kohl-Watzinger, p. 204 ff. Orfali's arguments[2] for assigning the synagogue of Capernaum to the early first century c.e. are unconvincing, and the conclusions drawn by him, at the close of his discussion, from Rabbinical sources are certainly unwarranted.[3]

H. C. Butler writes[4]:

'The characteristics of architectural style under Roman influence during the third century in parts of Syria are most pronounced. The buildings of Baalbek and Palmyra are magnificent illustrations of these tendencies—grandiose proportions, overelaboration of ornament, the covering of flat surfaces with elaborate carving, the use of unstructural features, such as consoles that have nothing to support, and the general lack of precision in the execution of small details, the aim being to secure a rich and imposing effect from a distance, rather than one that would bear minute examination.'

To a certain extent this verdict will be seen to be applicable to contemporary synagogue architecture in Palestine as well.

[1] That discovered by E. Renan (*Mission de Phénicie*, p. 774) at Kasiun is not a synagogue inscription (*v.* Kohl-Watzinger, op. cit., p. 209 f.). For the dated mosaic inscription of the Beth Alpha synagogue, see below, p. 77.

[2] G. Orfali, *Capharnaüm et ses ruines*, pp. 67 ff.

[3] He is right, however, in rejecting the idea of an Imperial founder (p. 82).

[4] *Publications of an American Archaeological Expedition to Syria in 1899–1900*, Part II, Architecture and other Arts, New York, 1903, p. 73.

A second period of synagogue building in Palestine was the fifth century. The criterion for assigning a synagogue to the first or the second period is the presence of the special receptacle for the Ark built in the wall of the orientation. Concomitant with the latter feature are the doors built not in the orientation side but in another one and the replacement of the elaborate mural decorations by mosaic art.[1]

7. *Inscriptions.*

As in the Diaspora so in Palestine, in many of the ancient synagogues inscriptions have been found. They are engraved upon lintels or pillars whose donors they commemorate, upon the railing of the Ark, and in one case upon the *kathedra*. Inscriptions are especially frequent in the mosaic floors of synagogues excavated since the war. The language is preponderantly Aramaic, the vernacular of Palestine at the period, and Greek. The relatively large number of known inscriptions of this nature includes only a few Hebrew ones.

Inscriptions on parts of the building are as a rule short, and limited to the honourable mention of the donor and the nature of his donation. Sometimes a blessing upon the donor is added, or the inscription may begin or end with a blessing upon the synagogue or Israel in general. Sometimes it consists of the donor's name alone. Occasionally the inscription is accompanied by a representation of a seven-branched candlestick, a ram's horn, or the like.

Outstanding in many respects among these ordinary inscriptions is the Greek one discovered by R. Weill in his excavation of the Ophel.[2] It dates from the century preceding the destruction of Jerusalem, and is therefore the oldest synagogue inscription found in Palestine. As there

---

[1] On the latter, *v.* p. 27 ff.

[2] R. Weill, *La Cité de David, Compte rendu des fouilles exécutées à Jérusalem, sur le site de la ville primitive. Campagne de 1913–14*, Paris, 1920, i, p. 186 ff., ii, Pl. XXV *a*.

is a rich literature on it[1] we shall here confine ourselves to
the text and a translation (Pl. XVI a).

1. Θεόδοτος Ούεττηνοῦ ἱερεὺς καὶ
2. ἀρχισυνάγωγος υἱὸς ἀρχισυν[αγώ-]
3. γ[ο]υ υἱωνὸς ἀρχισυν[α]γώγου ᾠκο-
4. Δόμησε τὴν συναγωγ[ὴ]ν εἰς ἀν[άγ]νω-
5. σ[ιν] νόμου καὶ εἰς [Δ]ιΔαχ[ὴ]ν ἐντολῶν καὶ
6. τὸν ξενῶνα κα[ὶ τὰ] Δώματα καὶ τὰ χρη-
7. σ[τ]ήρια τῶν ὑΔάτων εἰς κατάλυμα τοῖ-
8. ς [χ]ρῄзουσιν ἀπὸ τῆς ξέ[ν]ης, ἣν ἐθεμε-
9. λ[ίω]σαν οἱ πατέρες [α]ὐτοῦ καὶ οἱ πρε-
10. σ[β]ύτεροι καὶ Σιμων[ί]Δης

'Theodotos, son of Vettenos, Priest and Archisynagogos, son of
an Archisynagogos, grandson of an Archisynagogos, built the
synagogue for the reading of the Law and for the teaching of the
Commandments; furthermore, the Hospice and the Chambers,
and the water installation for lodging of needy strangers. The
foundation stone thereof had been laid by his fathers, and the
Elders, and Simonides.'

Nothing further is known about the persons here named,
but we may assume that they were Jews from the Diaspora.
The name Vettenos, obviously derived from that of the
Roman *gens Vettena*, has led many scholars to connect this
edifice with the 'Synagogue of the Libertines', *Acts* 6: 9; but
while this is not impossible, it cannot be proved.

An example of an inscription commemorating the donation of a part of a building is the Hebrew legend on the
portal (Pl. XVI b) of the little synagogue at Kafr Bir'im in
Upper Galilee.[2]

[1] Clermont-Ganneau, 'Une synagogue de l'époque hérodienne à
Jérusalem', *CAIL*, 1920, p. 187 f.; Th. Reinach, 'L'inscription de
Théodotos', *REJ*, vol. lxxi (1920), pp. 46 ff.; H. Vincent, 'Découverte
de la "synagogue des affranchis" à Jérusalem', *RB*, 1921, pp. 247 ff.;
S. A. Cook, *PEF. Q. St.*, 1921, pp. 22 ff.; H. Lietzmann, *ZNW*, 1921,
pp. 171 ff.; A. Deissmann, *Licht vom Osten*, 4. Aufl., Tübingen, 1923,
pp. 378 ff.
[2] W. G. Masterman, *Studies in Galilee*, p. 118, says that on his first
visit to this place in 1893 the portal was still standing, but on revisiting
it in 1907 he no longer found it there. A fragment of one of the

יהי שלום במקום הזה ובכל מקומות ישראל יוסה הלוי בן לוי עשה השקוף הזה
תבא ברכה במע(ש)יו של[ום][1] 'May there be peace in this Place[2]
and in all the Places[2] of Israel. Jose the Levite, the son of
Levi, made this lintel. May blessing come upon his deeds.
Peace.'[3]

At Capernaum, too, there are two inscriptions, the one
Greek and the other Aramaic, which tell of donations of
columns. The former was engraved on a column (Pl.
XVII *a*) in the interior of the synagogue (it has now been
incorporated in the restoration of the Franciscans) and
reads:

Text.[4]	Translation.
1. Ἡρώδης Μο[νι or, κι]	Herod, son of Mo[ni- or, Moki-]
2. μοῦ καὶ Ἰοῦστος	mos and Justos
3. υἱὸς ἅμα τοῖς	his son, together with the
4. τέκνοις ἔκτι-	children erect-
5. σαν	ed
6. τὸν κίονα	this column.

door-posts, however, was still lying near this spot on my visit there in
1929. A part of the inscription is still extant and is kept in the Louvre
Museum, Paris, *v.* R. Dussaud, *Les monuments palestiniens et judaïques*,
Paris, 1912, p. 85 f., Fig. N. 116.

[1] This inscription is already mentioned by two medieval Jewish
pilgrims, R. Samuel b. R. Samson (1210) and the Anonymous Pilgrim
of Livorno (1521), and was copied exactly, while still *in situ*, by E.
Renan.

[2] It is interesting to note that these inscriptions almost invariably
designate the synagogues by the Hebrew, Aramaic, or Greek word for
'place' (τόπος, אתרה, מקום).

[3] The hitherto accepted reading is במעיוש, which is explained as
due to the engraver's having written the ש of שיו, which he had
inadvertently omitted after the ע, at the end of the word. The omission
of a letter is quite a common occurrence in inscriptions, but to restore
it after the two following letters have been written seems a particularly
unintelligent thing for an engraver to do. As a matter of fact, the
facsimile of Renan (*op. cit.*, Pl. LXX, 1) shows clearly that the ש is
followed by a ל, and these two letters are certainly the beginning of
the word שלום, with which such inscriptions often close.

[4] G. Orfali, *JPOS*, 1926, pp. 159 ff.; id., *Antonianum*, 1926, pp.
407 ff.

The other, Aramaic, inscription, apparently of later date (Pl. XVII *b*), is interesting for the names it contains. The text is as follows:[1]

1.	חלפו בר זבידה בר יוחנן	ḤLPW, the son of Zebida, the son of Johanan,
2.	עבד הרן עמודה	made this column.
3.	ח]ה[י לא]ן(=לה) ברכתה	May blessing be his.

The last name in l. 1 is of course 'John'. Neither, however, can there be any doubt that the first two are Semitic originals of the New Testament ᾿Αλφαῖος and Ζεβεδαῖος. We know from other sources that Capernaum was still a Jewish town in Byzantine times, to which this inscription is no doubt to be assigned.

Interesting names and titles also occur in the following pillar inscription from a synagogue in Beth Gubrin (Beit Jibrin).[2]

Text.	*Translation.*
1.	דכיר	Remembered be
2.	למב קורים	for good Kyris[3]
3.	. . . עיי (?) ניח נפ[ש]	. . ., peace upon his soul,
4.	בר אוכסנטיס	the son of Auxentios
5.	דיבן (?) הדין עמודא	who built (?) this column
6.	ליקרה דכנישתא	in honour of the synagogue.
7.	שלום	Peace.

Less laconical than the preceding, no doubt by reason of the wider space available, are the mosaic inscriptions in synagogues of the Byzantine period.

The first considerable number of inscriptions to be found together were those in the mosaic floor of the synagogue of Naʿaran (ʿAin Dûk).[4] Despite a good deal of philological treatment, some of them have not yet yielded a final

---

[1] G. Orfali, *Antonianum*, 1926, pp. 401 ff.; E. L. Sukenik, *ZDPV*, 1932, pp. 75 ff.

[2] E. L. Sukenik, 'A Synagogue Inscription from Beit Jibrin', *JPOS*, 1930, pp. 76 ff.; ibid., 1932, Klein, p. 271; ibid., Sukenik, p. 272.

[3] For this title, cf. now Appendix 2, p. 82.

[4] *v.* p. 6 n. 2, p. 28 ff.

satisfactory reading and interpretation, so that it may be worth while to deal with them here at greater length.

The first inscription, which was exposed accidentally by the bursting of a shell in 1918, is situated in the third panel of the floor from the entrance, in the midst of the pictorial representation of Daniel already described (*v.* p. 30), between Daniel and the lion on his right hand (Pl. XVIII *a*). It was first published in 1919, and has since been a *crux interpretum*. I venture to propose the following solution.

1.	דכיר לטב
2.	בינימין פרנסה
3.	בר יוסה
4.	[ד]כירין לטב כל מן
5.	[ד]מתחזק ויהב או
6.	[די]הב בהדן אתרה
7.	[ק]דישה בן דהב בן
8.	[כ]סף בן כל מקמה
9.	[ד]היא [ואיתו]ן חו(ל)קהון
10.	בהדן אתרה קדישה
11.	אמן

'(1) Remembered be for good (2) Benjamin the Parnas (3) the son of Jose. (4) Remembered be for good any one (5) that shall lend his support and give, or (6) has given, to this Holy (7) Place, either gold or (8) silver or any precious thing (9) whatsoever; or any that have brought their contribution (10) to this Holy Place. (11) Amen.'

The above departs from the accepted interpretation only in respect of line 9, for which the following restorations have been proposed.

1. Clermont-Ganneau: ל[ה יא]הרו[ן] חוקהון 'they shall not delay their dues.'

It seems obvious, however, that the object of all such inscriptions is to honour the memory of voluntary, including prospective, donors, whereas 'delay' is only possible where obligatory dues are concerned.

2. Vincent and Carrière: ל[ה יא]ובדו[ן] חוקהון 'they shall not lose their share.'

The same objection applies to this as the preceding.

3. Klein: י[הוא] להו[ן] חו(ל)קהון 'they shall have their share.'

This reading is, to begin with, graphically impossible, as the second letter is unmistakably ׳, not ׀. But it also involves a conception that is foreign to Jewish tradition and sentiment. A synagogue is not the property of a limited number of partners who acquire their respective interests in it in virtue of their contributions. The synagogue has always belonged to the community, and been open to every Jew wherever he came from. There are even instances of communities coercing their members to contribute towards the building of a synagogue, and conversely individuals have of their own accord built synagogues and donated them to their communities. What individuals of the latter sort, or any of the donors commemorated in our inscriptions, thereby secured was 'a share in the world to come' or 'a lot together with the Righteous', as it is put in the *kathedra* inscription dealt with above (p. 60 n. 2), but not proprietary rights in the synagogue.

Prof. Klein is, however, right in correcting the חוקהון of the mosaicist to חולקהון, which occurs in another inscription from the same place. Inasmuch, however, as in our inscriptions this word follows upon a list of various kinds of donations, it most plausibly means 'contributions' (literally 'shares'), and no doubt that is its meaning in the other text too.

In this benediction upon all and sundry who have rendered or may render any material service to the synagogue, we have clearly a prototype of the well-known prayer מי שברך which is still recited in the synagogue every Sabbath morning.[1]

---

[1] In order to facilitate comparison, we append a translation of this prayer herewith: 'He who blessed our Fathers Abraham, Isaac, and Jacob, may he bless all this holy congregation together with all the holy congregations—them, and their wives, and their sons, and their daughters, and all their belongings. Also all those that give synagogues for prayer and those that come thither to pray, and those that give lamps for lighting and wine for Qiddush and Habdalah and bread to strangers and charity to the poor, and all those that engage in communal work conscientiously—may the Holy One, blessed be He, give unto them their reward, and remove all sickness from them and heal

Of other mosaic inscriptions of Na'aran whose exegesis is still capable of improvement, we select the following for the sake of the realia specified therein. It is in the floor of the vestibule.

1. דכיר לטב פינחס כהנה בר יוסטה דיהב
2. טימי   פסיפסה
3. מן דידה   ומרי[ו?]ש[ת]ה[?]

'(1) Remembered be for good Phineas the Priest the son of Justos who gave (2) the price of this mosaic (3) and this basin from his substance.'

The crux of this text is the last word ומרישת, two of the letters of which can, as we have indicated, be read in more than one way. The scholars who have written on this inscription are almost unanimous in connecting our word with מריש, 'beam' (for the number is certainly singular). But it is hardly likely that a man would contribute a mosaic floor and one beam. My translation 'basin' is founded on the following passage in the Palestinian Talmud (*Terum.* 45 d): 'R. Jannai was exceedingly afraid of it (i.e. of the serpent) and used to stand his bed in four מרשין of water.'

The *Arukh* renders 'and used to suspend his bed by four ropes, moistened with water', taking מרושין to be the familiar Babylonian-Aramaic word מורשא; which may in places be the equivalent of Syriac ܚܒܠܐ 'rope' but never, so far as I know, occurs in Palestinian sources. On the other hand, Levy's explanation[1] of our מרושין as 'vessels', is supported by a similar passage in *b. Ta'anith* 21 a: ' . . . and the legs of his bed stood in four buckets (ספלים) of water in order to prevent the ants from climbing upon him'.

Difficulties in the reading of mosaic inscriptions may often be due to damages in the floor having been repaired without all their bodies, and forgive all their iniquities, and send blessing and prosperity in all the works of their hands, together with all their brethren Israel. And let us say, Amen.'

For other epigraphic parallels to the phraseology of this prayer, cf. the Kafr Bir'im inscription cited above (p. 71) and the Ḥammath-by-Gadara inscription, Appendix, 2, p. 82.

[1] *Wörterbuch über die Talmudim und Midraschim*, s.v.

much regard to the sense of the writing. This is clearly what has happened in the case of another Naʿaran inscription[1] which now looks something as follows (Pl. XVIII *b*):

דכי

1. דיר לטב מרות [. . . . . ק] טינה ויע[?]יר
2. ברה דהנון מתחזקין בה[דן] אתרה
3. (blank) יין בהרן אתר[ה קריש[ה א[מן]
4.

It is evident from the different size of the *tesserae* that everything between l. 1 and the extant part of l. 4 is secondary. The repairing mosaicist, instead of continuing l. 1 from the undamaged part, began anew with דכיר, but carelessly omitted the כ, and instead of so laying out the letters as to finish with l. 4, introduced בהרן אתרה unnecessarily in l. 3. Lines 1 and 4, which are original, are straight and parallel with the borders of the inscription; ll. 2–3, the work of the repairer, are uneven.

A very frequent formula in synagogue inscriptions is 'Remembered be for good X (and Y) who made this column (or lintel, or mosaic panel).' No doubt the donors, rather than the workmen, are meant. In one case, however, it is explicitly the latter who receive honourable mention. In the mosaic floor of the Beth Alpha synagogue near the entrance, we read

1. ΜΝΙϹΘΟΥϹΙΝΥΤЄ
2. ΧΝΙΤЄΥΚΑΜΝΟΝ
3. ΤЄϹΤѠЄΡΓΟΝΤΟΥ
4. ΤѠΜΑΡΙΑΝΟϹΚΑΙ
5. ΑΝΙΝΑϹΥΟϹ

the spelling of which may be corrected as follows:

Μνησθῶσιν οἱ τεχνῖται οἱ κάμνοντες τὸ ἔργον τοῦτο Μαριανὸς καὶ Ἀνίνας υἱός.

[1] H. Lietzmann, *ZNW*. 1921, pp. 252 ff., ascribes all its linguistic anomalies to the incompetence of the mosaicist. S. Klein, ידיעות המכון למדעי היהדות, vol. ii, p. 40 f., reads l. 1 and the beginning of l. 2 (decidedly against the *ductus literarum* of this text) as one word דכירין and in l. 4 restores יהוא חול[קהון]. The objection to יהוא חולקהון is that in none of the numerous other inscriptions of Naʿaran is the same person honoured with more than one blessing.

The sense is accordingly: 'May the craftsmen who carried out this work, Marianos and his son Ḥanina, be held in remembrance.'

This is the only Greek inscription in this synagogue, and is no doubt entirely due to the initiative of the mosaicists themselves. They were evidently Greek-speaking Jews from abroad, and this may account for the clumsiness of the Aramaic letters in some of the other inscriptions, which were presumably executed by the one with less Jewish education. In the earlier synagogue of Gerasa, on the contrary, there is only one modest Aramaic inscription in one of the aisles:

	Text.	*Translation.*
1.	שלום על כל	Peace upon all
2.	ישראל אמן אמן	Israel Amen Amen
3.	סלה פינחס בר	Selah. Phinehas son of
4.	ברוך יוסה בר	Baruch, Jose son of
5.	שמואל וי(ו)דן בר חזקיה	Samuel, and Judan son of Hezekiah.

Although nothing further is told us about these persons, we may, since their merits would certainly have been stated had they been donors, conclude that they were the mosaicists, who were not suffered here, as in the rural synagogue of Beth Alpha, to perpetuate their memory in a large legend in the most prominent part of the floor. Here, then, we have Aramaic-speaking mosaicists in the synagogue of a hellenized community.

Finally, mention should be made of the only dated synagogue inscription. It is one of the mosaic floor inscriptions of the Beth Alpha synagogue of which another specimen has just been dealt with (p. 76). The first two lines of it read, translated, as follows: 'This mosaic was laid down in the [. . . .] year of the reign of the Emperor Justin.'

This is the only dated inscription which the ancient synagogues of Palestine have thus far yielded, and is therefore a valuable aid in determining the age of other ruins of the same type.[1]

[1] For further particulars see my *Beth Alpha*, pp. 50 ff.

In the preceding chapters, I have tried to give a survey of the present state of research on ancient synagogues. The picture would have been more satisfactory had I been able to give a full description of the many monuments that have thus far been discovered, particularly in Palestine, but that would have exceeded the scope of these lectures. The exploration of these monuments has not yet been completed. New discoveries are constantly being made, in Palestine as well as in the centres of the Diaspora, which will undoubtedly add new details to our conception of the early synagogues. But even now we may safely predict that these details will not change the conception as a whole.

As in so many other spheres of Jewish spiritual life so in the synagogue, the idea did not engender original material forms. The form, the subject of the present lectures, was borrowed by Jewry from the outer world. It was a convenient form and lasted for several centuries, spreading over many countries. With a changed environment, the appearance of the synagogues also changed. There is therefore no Jewish style of architecture to be looked for in the structures described here, and no form normative for millennia. What we have seen was good for a given period; other generations gave other material shape to the old idea.

APPENDIX

FOUR interesting discoveries in the field of synagogue research that have taken place since the reading of these lectures are worth describing briefly here.

1. *The Synagogue of Stobi.*[1]

In the year 1931, Dr. Jozo Petrović, Custodian of the National Museum, Beograd, in his excavations of the ancient thermal baths at Stobi,[2] Yugoslavia, brought to light a structure the description and plan of which are immediately reminiscent of the synagogue of Beth Alpha.

The building is oriented to the east, as we have already seen to be the case with synagogues in countries west of Palestine. It consists of a basilica 19·20 m. by 14·20 m., divided by two rows of pillars into a nave 7·40 m. wide and two aisles each 2·60 m. wide. From the eastern wall of the nave projects an apse. In front of the basilica is a vestibule 3·75 m. wide, from which three doorways, a wider one in the middle and two narrower ones at the sides, lead into the nave and the aisles respectively. On the opposite side of the vestibule are three other doors, of which the southernmost leads into a small chamber 4 m. by 3·40 m. (where 170 copper coins of the fifth century were found), and the other two into an atrium. The atrium is surrounded on four sides by a covered colonnade, and in the south-east corner of the peristyle stands a marble basin for ritual purposes. On the south side the atrium communicates by doors with two other small rooms.

From the type of synagogue, I should not be inclined to date it earlier than the end of the fourth century.

Of special interest is an inscription of thirty-two lines on one of the columns, which reads as follows:

1. [ΚΛ.] Τιβέριος Πολύ-
2. χαρμος ὁ καὶ ʼΑχύρι-
3. ος ὁ πατὴρ τῆς ἐν
4. Στόβοις συναγωγῆς
5. ὃς πολειτ▨ευσάμε-
6. νος πᾶσαν πολειτεί-

---

[1] The first report of this discovery appeared in the Jewish newspaper *Židov*, Zagreb, of 9 June 1932, p. 3 f. An account was then published in *Starinar*, the organ of the Serbian Archaeological Society, 1932, pp. 81 ff., by the excavator, Dr. Jozo Petrović.

[2] Στόβοι, a famous town in Paeonia, near Monastir.

7. αν κατὰ τὸν ᾿Ιουδαϊ-
8. σμὸν εὐχῆς ἕνεκεν
9. τοὺς μὲν οἴκους τῷ
10. ἁγίῳ τόπῳ καὶ τὸ
11. τρίκλεινον σὺν τῷ
12. τετραστόῳ ἐκ τῶν
13. οἰκείων χρημάτων
14. μηδὲν ὅλως παραψά-
15. μενος τῶν ἁγίων. Τὴν
16. δὲ ἐξουσίαν τῶν ὑπε-
17. ρῴων πάντων πᾶσαν
18. καὶ τὴν δεσποτείαν
19. ἔχειν ἐμὲ τὸν Κλ. Τιβέρι-
20. ον Πολύχαρμον [[καὶ τοὺς]]
21. καὶ τοὺς κληρονόμους
22. τοὺς ἐμοὺς διὰ παντὸς
23. βίου. Ὅς ἂν δὲ βουληθῇ
24. τι καινοτομῆσαι παρὰ τὰ ὑ-
25. π᾿ ἐμοῦ δοχθέντα δώσει τῷ
26. πατριάρχῃ δηναρίων (μ)υριά-
27. δας εἴκοσι πέντε. Οὕτω γάρ
28. μοι συνέδοξεν. Τὴν δὲ ἐπι-
29. σκευὴν τῆς κεράμου τῶν
30. ὑπερῴων ποιεῖσθαι ἐμὲ
31. καὶ κληρονόμους
32. ἐμούς.

The following translation, which differs from that of Dr. Petrović in a few details, was arrived at after study by my colleague Dr. M. Schwabe and myself: '(I) Claudios Tiberios Polycharmos, also named Achyrios, Father of the Congregation at Stobi, who conducted my whole life according to Judaism, (have), in fulfilment of a vow, (erected) the buildings for the Holy Place and the triklinion together with the tetrastoon with my own means without in the least touching the sacred (funds). Howbeit, the right of disposal of all the upper chambers and the proprietorship (thereof) shall be vested in me, Claudios Tiberios Polycharmos, and my heirs for life; and whosoever shall seek in any way to alter any of these dispositions of mine shall pay unto the Patriarch two hundred and fifty thousand denarii. For thus have I resolved. But the repair of the tile-roof of the upper chambers shall be carried out by me and my heirs.'[1]

[1] The inscription was meanwhile also published, and briefly com-

2. *Ḥammath-by-Gadara.*

An important addition was recently made to the small number of synagogues with mosaic floors known in Palestine. Discovered by officers of the Department of Antiquities of the Palestine Government early in 1932, this site at the famous hot springs by the Yarmuk near Gadara was excavated by the writer in November of that year on behalf of the Hebrew University, Jerusalem. The structure was found to consist of the synagogue proper with several annexes on the east side, and to have a narrow courtyard on its south and west sides. The basilica was approximately square in shape, measuring about 13 m. by 13 m. Though situated east of the Jordan it is orientated not to the west but, like the synagogues north of Jerusalem in Cisjordania, to the south. Accordingly, the two dividing rows of columns run from north to south. The nave is 7·80 m. wide and the eastern and western aisle 3 m. and 2·40 m. respectively. The two main rows of columns are joined at the north end by a third at a distance of 1·80 m. from the north wall. The narrow aisles running continuously around three sides of the nave are reminiscent of the architecture of the Chorazin and Capernaum synagogues. There are still remnants of the benches that lined the walls.

At the south wall is a platform containing a few steps leading up to the apse which was occupied by the Ark of the Law. The space devoted to the Ark was divided off from the rest of the building by a marble screen, of which some small posts and slabs, partly engraved with Greek inscriptions, were found.

The mosaic floor has not been very well preserved, but the design of the nave, at any rate, can be reconstructed with certainty. It is surrounded by a guilloche and a wavy border and divided into three panels, which are likewise framed in a guilloche. The first panel from the apse contains in its centre an Aramaic inscription of ten lines within a wreath with a lemniscus, flanked by a lion and a cypress on either side. At the top of the second panel are mented upon, by H. Lietzmann in *Z.N.W.* xxxii, 1933, p. 93 f. Obviously Lietzmann had not at his disposal the photographs which we were able to use. On that account our reproduction is, in some places, different and more accurate. For πολειτευσάμενος πᾶσαν πολειτείαν κατὰ τὸν ʼΙουΔαϊσμόν Lietzmann, *l.c.*, brings two excellent parallels. This expression seems, moreover, as my colleague Dr. Schwabe points out, to have been favoured among Jewish writers for designating Jewish life according to the Jewish Law, cf. Joseph. *Ant.* xii. 142, *Vita* 12; 2 *Macc.* 6: 1, 11: 25, 3 *Macc.* 3: 4, 4 *Macc.* 2: 8.

two long inscriptions enclosed in one *tabula ansata*, the remainder of this panel being filled with intersecting squares containing flowers and pomegranates. The third panel consists mainly of geometrical designs and had originally two inscriptions, of which only one remains now.

The inscriptions as usual invoke blessings upon donors, but differ from those we have thus far been dealing with in specifying the amounts of money contributed. Especially important are the references to Jews of other towns, including Capernaum. The names and titles in the inscription of the first panel illustrate particularly well the extent to which Jews in the neighbourhood of the Decapolis tended to become hellenized. The text is given herewith:

1.	ודכיר לטב
2.	קורס הופלים וקורה
3.	פרוטון וקורס סלוסטיס
4.	חתנה וקומס פרורוס ברה
5.	וקורים פוטייס חתנה וקורס
6.	חנינה ברה הננון ובניהון
7.	דמיצוותון תדירן בכל אתר
8.	דהבון הכה חמישה דינרין
9.	דהב מלך עלמה יתן ברכתה
10.	בעמלהון אמן אמן סלה

'And remembered be for good Kyris Hoples, and Kyra Proton, and Kyris Sallustius his son-in-law, and Comes Phroros his son, and Kyris Photios his son-in-law, and Kyris Ḥanina his son— they, and their children—whose acts of charity are constant everywhere [and] who have given here five golden denarii. May the King of the Universe give his blessing in their undertakings. Amen. Amen. Selah.'

From various indications, including the title of 'Comes', we may assign the erection of this synagogue to the first half of the fifth century, C.E. The archaeological evidence shows that it was ultimately destroyed and set on fire by angry attackers.

3. *Dura Europos.*

Dura Europos is situated on the right bank of the river Euphrates, on the road leading from Aleppo to Baghdad. The excavation of this site was resumed in 1928 by the Joint Expedition of Yale University and the French Academy of Inscriptions. At the end of 1932, under the direction of Prof. C. Hopkins and the Comte du Mesnil du Buisson, an ancient synagogue was discovered—one of the most interesting of its kind. We may even regard it as the most remarkable find on record in the sphere of Jewish archaeology. A short visit to the place at the beginning of March 1933 enabled me, through the kindness of the director, to share with the excavators the pleasure of contemplating their most valuable find. A detailed account must be left to the discoverers, and will appear in due course when their work is completed. The object of the note I here append is merely to bring it to the attention of those interested, in anticipation of the official report.[1]

The synagogue was situated in a quarter near the main gate of the city on the west—a little to the north of it. A street ran in front of the synagogue and behind it was the city wall. The synagogue proper is a single room of about 13 by 7·60 metres, having on the east a courtyard with a peristyle. A niche built in the middle of its western wall and surmounted by a shell certainly served as the place where the Ark of the Law was laid when it was brought in for the services. It clearly shows that the orientation of the synagogue was to the west. This is in agreement with the general scheme of orientation of ancient synagogues, as described above (p. 50 ff.). Along the walls were benches for the worshippers. The entrance to the synagogue was through the courtyard on the east.

The outstanding feature of the synagogue is the large number of frescoes, mostly in good condition, which cover its inner walls. These frescoes represent a cycle of Biblical episodes, often depicting a scene in successive stages. On some of these panels Greek and Aramaic inscriptions indicating the nature of the scenes depicted, are still visible. Especially numerous are the pictures on the better preserved western wall, which still stands more than 5 metres high. Commencing with the frescoes round the aforementioned niche, there is a representation of the Torah shrine in the middle, with a seven-branched candlestick, a citrus fruit (*Ethrog*) and a palm branch (*Lulab*) on its left, and a representation of the sacrifice of Isaac on its right. Abraham is seen standing with his back to the spectator, holding in his right hand the upright knife, on the point of carrying out the divine command upon his son, who is lying bound on the altar near by. The divine intervention is portrayed by the hand, a familiar symbol of the power of God in both Christian and Jewish Biblical art (cf. above, p. 34). Abraham will now perceive the presence of the ram that is tied to a bush

[1] A paper on this discovery by Prof. Clark Hopkins was read before the French Academy of Inscriptions, Paris, by the Comte du Mesnil du Buisson on 2 June 1933.

behind him. On both sides of the niche are panels which have not yet been exposed, and we may eagerly look forward to the stories they have to tell. Of the panels above it, the most interesting are four, containing one figure each, of which I am inclined to identify the right two as Moses and the left two as Joshua. The upper right-hand picture presents the scene of Moses at the burning bush. He has already approached this amazing phenomenon, his shoes are already put off, and his right hand is outstretched in an attitude of astonishment and curiosity. His head is slightly raised and he is looking straight in front of him, attentively taking in the words spoken to him by God. It is a picture full of life and movement. Below this, separated by a wavy border, is a representation of an event which took place in a later period of his life. The surprise and astonishment, exhibited by the face and posture of the shepherd as he received his first divine mission, gives way to an expression of tranquillity and consciousness of the divine favour bestowed upon the leader and prophet at the height of his glory as he descends from Mount Sinai to deliver the words of God to his people. Moses is here depicted standing straight with his face to the spectator and holding an open scroll in his hands. The divine exaltation of the prophet is attested by the veil, in red colour, placed on a stand which is set on the floor at his right side. Of the upper left picture, only the lower part remains, and would be difficult to identify were it not for the fact that this part has preserved a pair of shoes seen standing on the ground, next to a pair of bare feet. The only other Biblical personage who was commanded to remove his shoes was Joshua, when the angel appeared to him before the siege of Jericho. We may therefore assume that this is a representation of that event. Below this picture Joshua is represented in connexion with another miracle, following the capture of Jericho. In this panel a man is seen standing upright holding his hands in an attitude of prayer, while above his head are the sun on his right and the moon on his left. Directly above his head stars are also visible. I think there could be no other interpretation of this picture than the miracle that happened to Joshua during his battle with the Amorite kings, when 'the sun stood still over Gibeon and the moon in the vale of Ajalon'.

On the same wall there is a picture of the Exodus, in three parts. Under the figure of Moses leading the Israelites out of Egypt there is an Aramaic inscription משה בר נפק מן מצרים 'Moses going out from Egypt'. A panel below it represents the restoration of the Ark from its captivity in the hands of the Philistines. On the right side of this panel the temple of Dagon is portrayed, showing the devastation caused by the presence of the Ark there. The images of the god are thrown down from their pedestals, while holy vessels and musical instruments lie strewn over the floor. On the left side is seen a cart drawn by cows, with the Ark of the Covenant placed upon it. Five persons are shown, who no doubt represent the five lords of the Philistines.

Other pictures on the wall show David playing his harp, Solomon's judgement, the dedication of the Tabernacle (with the high-priest Aaron, beside whose head is the word APωN), the story of Moses striking the rock (from which water gushes forth in 12 streams flowing towards the 12 tents in front of the Tabernacle, representing the camp of the 12 tribes of Israel). A number of other Biblical stories, such as Elijah's test offering on Mount Carmel, the resurrection of the child, visions of Zecharia, &c., are depicted on the other walls.

The value of this discovery is greatly enhanced by a dated Aramaic inscription found on one of the ceiling tiles, which says that 'this house was built in the year 565'. The era, as in all other inscriptions at Dura and Palmyra, is the Seleucidan, making the date 244 C.E. Since the city was destroyed not very long after the middle of the third century, this synagogue did not have a long existence. From the same inscription we learn that a certain Samuel the Priest (שמואל כהנה) held the office of Presbyter when this synagogue was built. The latter is mentioned again in a Greek inscription found on another tile of the ceiling, where he is called ΠΡΕϹΒΥΤΕΡΟϹ ΤωΝ ΙΟΥΔΕωΝ.

I do not intend to go into the many problems of the style of the frescoes nor their importance for the solution of some problems which were mentioned in the lectures (*vide* p. 67). Confirmation of the statement made in the lectures that the ancient synagogues had wall paintings and an idea of the nature of these paintings are unexpectedly supplied by this discovery.

4. *The Synagogue at 'Esfia on Mount Carmel.*

To the Palestinian synagogues which show the cycle of the Zodiac on their mosaic floors, like those at Na'aran and Beth Alpha, a third one may now be added, namely that of Esfia on Mount Carmel, which was excavated by the Department of Antiquities of the Government of Palestine in the beginning of 1933. Unfortunately, it was impossible to clear the entire area of the synagogue owing to its being partly covered by modern houses of the village. Only a little more than the northern half of it could be cleared.

Like the synagogue of Khirbet Semmaka referred to above

(p. 50), it faced west. Two rows, each of five pillars, 60 by 60 cm., divided it into the usual nave and two side aisles. It is almost a square building of 10·10 by 10·70 metres. The width of the nave is about 4·30 metres and that of the northern aisle 2·55 metres.

The greater part of the mosaic floor was damaged. The part which has survived shows that a border 1·50 metres wide, consisting of geometrical patterns, ran round the four sides of the floor. There are three small panels in the centre of the eastern side of this border, the middle panel containing an inscription שלום על ישראל—'Peace be upon Israel!' The two side panels had each a seven-branched candlestick, flanked on one side by a ram's horn (*shofar*) and a lectern, and on the other side by a citrus fruit (*Ethrog*) and a palm branch (*Lulab*). The floor of the nave was divided into three panels—two of them wide and one narrow, the latter being at the eastern end. The narrow panel contained an Aramaic inscription in a *tabula ansata*. The inscription is partly broken, but from what is left we may conclude that it invoked the usual blessing upon the benefactors. The panel west of the inscription consists of a vine-branch with leaves and clusters of grapes, with various kinds of birds among them pecking at the grapes. The part which has survived near the inscription shows the upper part of two peacocks facing each other. Only a small part of this panel remains. A little more is left of the next panel, which is a square enclosing two concentric circles. The diameter of the larger circle is 2·75 metres and that of the smaller one 1·35 metres. On the analogy of Naʿaran and Beth Alpha we may assume that the smaller circle contained a chariot of the Sun, of which almost nothing is left. In the space between the inner and outer circles there are remains of only five signs of the Zodiac. These were arranged clockwise. Of the sign of the first month of the spring—Aries—only the remains of the legs are visible. Very little is left of the sign of the last month of the winter—Pisces. The preceding month of the winter season—Aquarius—is here represented in the form of a pitcher. Of Capricorn only the ears are visible. One arm and a leg are the surviving parts of Sagittarius. On the upper left corner of the square a winged figure is visible, symbolizing one of the seasons of the year. Since no inscriptions accompany this season, we cannot know what season of the year it represents. This mosaic shows once more how prevalent the Zodiac was in the Jewish popular art of this period.

INDEX

Aaron the Priest, representation of, 85.
Abraham and Isaac, representation of, 34, 83 f.
Abun, R., 27 f.
Acre, 25.
Aegina, synagogue at, 44 f., 46, 51.
Agrippa (tetrarch), 64.
'Ain Dûk (Na'aran), synagogue at, 6, 28 ff., 32, 34, 65, 72 ff., 85 f.
Albright, W. F., viii.
Aleppo, synagogue at, 57.
Alexandria, synagogues at, 1, 46, 48[1].
Altar, pictorial representation of, 34, 36, 83.
Anderson, 4.
Angels, 38[1].
Annexed Chambers, v. Synagogue.
Antoninus, 63.
Apion, 51.
Apotropaic, v. Motives.
Apse, v. Synagogue.
Aquarius, v. Zodiac.
Aramaic, v. Inscriptions.
Arch of Titus, 63.
Aries, v. Zodiac.
Ark of the Law, 17[2], 18 f., 24, 27, 43, 52 ff., 69, 81, 83.
— pictorial representation of, 20, 30 f., 35, 53 ff., 83.
— railing of, 57, 69.
— veil of, 35, 56 f.
Art, Christian, 67, 83; Graeco-Roman, 67; Jewish, 67, 83, 86; mosaic, 27 f., 69; mural, 11 f., 16 f., 22, 68.
Ascalon, 57.
Ashdod, 57.
Astral, v. Motives.

Baalbek, 68.
Babylonia, 1, 49.
Bacher, W., 59[1].
Basin, 75, 79.
Beisan, 31.
Beit Jibrin, v. Beth Gubrin.
Bema, 32, 57.
Benches, v. Synagogue.
Benjamin of Tudela, 3[1].
Berliner, A., 3[1].
Beth Alpha, synagogue at, 6, 31 ff., 48, 55 ff., 65, 76 f., 85 f.
Beth Gubrin (Beit Jibrin), synagogue at, 72.
Biblical, v. Motives.

Biq'ath Beth Netopha, 27.
Birt, Th., 53[1].
British School of Archaeology, Jerusalem, excavations of, 6, 35 ff.
Buber, S., 48[1].
Building materials, v. Synagogue.
Butler, H. C., 68.

Caesar, Julius, 42.
Caesars, Antonine and Severan, 62.
Candelabrum, donation of, 63.
Candlesticks, seven-branched, pictorial representation of, 17[1], 20, 28, 31, 35, 37, 43, 55 f., 63, 69, 84, 86.
Capernaum, synagogue at, 5, 7 ff., 50, 52, 55 f., 65, 68, 71 f., 81.
Capricorn, v. Zodiac.
Carmel, Mount, synagogues on, 50, 85 f.
Carmoli, E., 3[1].
Carrière, Père B., 6[2], 73.
Carruca, 17[2].
Catacombs at Rome, 53, 67.
Ceiling tiles, v. Synagogue.
Chamber of Hewn Stone, 46.
Chariot of the Sun, representation of, 29, 34, 86.
Chebar, river, 50[1].
Chorazin (Keraze), synagogue at, 5 f., 21 ff., 52, 56, 58, 60, 65, 81.
Cisjordania, v. Place Names.
Clermont-Ganneau, 27[2], 70[1], 73.
Coins, 79.
Conder, 4.
Congregation, blessings on, 37, 74[1], 36.
Cook, S. A., 17[2], 70[1].
Crowfoot, J. W., 6[5].
Cyclades, 37.

Daniel, prayer of, 51; in the lion's den, representation of, 30, 73.
Dating of synagogues, v. Synagogue.
David, representation of, 85.
Decapolis, 82.
Deissmann, A., 42[2], 70[1].
Delos, seat of Moses at, 61; synagogue at, 37 ff., 42, 46, 50.
Deutsche Orient-Gesellschaft, excavations of, 4 f., 8, 21.
Diaspora, synagogues in, 1, 37 ff., 46, 48[1], 49 ff., 51, 57, 61, 69, 79 f., 82 ff.
Dikkeh, synagogue at, 25.
Diplostoon (Alexandria) 46, 48[1].

Dominican Fathers, excavations of, 6, 28 ff.
Donations and donors, 44, 62 f., 69 ff., 79 f., 82, 86.
Dura Europos, synagogue at, 82 ff.
Dussaud, R., 70[2].

École Biblique et Archéologique Française, Jerusalem, excavations of, v. Dominican Fathers.
École Française, Athens, excavations of, 37.
Egypt, synagogues, 1, 46, 48[1], 51.
Eleazar b. R. Simeon, R., 64[1].
Eleazar b. R. Zadok, R., 64.
Elijah's Test, representation of, 85.
Entrance, v. Synagogue.
Epstein, J. N., 27, 60[2].
Esdraelon, valley of, 6.
'Esfia, synagogue at, 85 f.
Eusebius, 47, 65.
Ezekiel, vision of, 17[2], 63.

Figures, animals, etc., v. Motives.
Finkelstein, L., 1[1].
Flood, representation of, 35.
Floor, v. Synagogue.
Forecourt of the Temple, people's, 47, women's, 47.
Franciscan Fathers, excavations of, 5, 7, 8, 20, 71.
French Government, explorations of, 4.
Frescoes, v. Synagogue.
Funds of Synagogue, v. Synagogue.

Galilee, synagogues, 4, 5, 7 ff., 31 ff., 50, 61 f., 68, 70 ff., 76 f., 85 f.
Gallery, v. Synagogue.
Gamaliel, Patriarch, 64.
Gennesareth, Sea of, 7.
Geometrical figures, v. Motives.
Gerasa, v. Jerash.
Gerkan, A. von, 40[1].
German excavations, 4 f., 8, 21, 27, 40, 42, 44.
Gibeon, representation of Miracle at, 84.
Ginsberg, H. L., vii, 48[1].
Glass, gilt, 17[2], 53, 54, 56, 57.
— lamp, representation of, 31.
Gollancz, Israel, viii.
Goell, Th., viii.
Greek Lands, synagogues in, 1, 37 ff., 49 f.
Guérin, V., 4.
Guest room, v. Synagogue.

Halicarnassus, 49.
Hamilton, R. W., 6.[5]
Ḥammath by Gadara, synagogue at, 7[2], 81 f.
Ḥammath by Tiberias, seat of Moses at, 59; seven-branched candlestick at, 55; synagogue at, 6, 20.
Hananiah, R., 64.
Hebrew University, excavations of, 6, 31 f., 81 f.
Heliopolis, 51.
Herodian Temple, 63.
Herzfeld, E., 57.
Hiller, E., 5.
Hoffmann, D., 3[1].
Hölscher, 5.
Hopkins, C., 82.
Human figures, v. Motives.

Iconoclasm, 16, 18, 21, 25, 62, 65.
Iconostasis, 57.
Inscriptions, 4, 49, 60, 62, 69 ff., 73 ff.
— Aramaic, 28, 37, 60, 72 ff., 77, 81, 85 f.
— dated, 69, 77, 85.
— Greek, 37, 38, 40, 42, 44, 69 f., 71, 76 f., 79 f., 81, 85.
— Hebrew, 3, 29 f., 34, 57, 70 f., 77.
Isaac, representation of sacrifice of, 34, 83.
Ish-Shalom (Friedman), M., 48[1].
Islam, 2.
Israel, Land of, 52.

Jannai, R., 75.
Japhet, representation of, 36.
Jerash, synagogue at, 6, 35 ff., 55, 65, 77.
Jericho, representation of miracle of Joshua at, 84.
Jerome, 65.
Jerusalem, synagogues at, 46, 69 f.; Temple at, 47, 51 f., 55, 57.
Jewish cycle, v. Motives.
Jewish Palestine Exploration Society, excavations of, 6, 55.
Jewish Supreme Court, 46.
Josephus, 7, 37, 42, 49, 51[1], 64, 66.
Juda han-Nasi, R., 17[2].
Juster, J., 47[1].
Justin, Emperor, 77.
Justus of Tiberias, 64.

Kafr Bir'im, synagogue at, 24 ff., 70 f.
Kafr Kanna, synagogue at, 27.
Kalir, 66.

Kasiun, 68[1].
Kathedra, *v.* Seat of Moses.
Keraze, *v.* Chorazin.
Kitchener, H. H., 4, 62.
Klein, S., 72[2], 73 f.
Klostermann, 65[1].
Kohl, H., 5, 8, 27[1], 62[1], 68[1].
Krauss, S., 1[1], 46[1].

Lamps, 31, 55, 74[1].
Lectern, 37, 53 ff., 86.
Levy, J., 75.
Libertines, synagogue of, 70.
Lietzmann, H., 70[1], 76[1], 80[1].
Löw, L., 63[1].

Magic symbols in art, *v.* Motives.
Marmorstein, A., 60[1].
Masterman, E. W. G., 70[2].
Mayer, L. A., vii.
Menes, A., 1[1].
Menorah, *v.* Candlestick.
Mesnil du Buisson, Comte du, 82.
Miletus, synagogue at, 40 ff., 46, 50 f.
Moore, G. F., 2[1].
Mosaic floor, *v.* Synagogue.
— inscriptions, *v.* Inscriptions.
— repair, 75 f.
— workmanship, 35, 44.
Mosaicists, commemoration of, 76 f.
Moses, 51; representation of, 84; seat of, 24, 38, 57 ff., 69, 74.
Mosque al-Ḥayyât, Aleppo, 57.
Motives in synagogue art:
  animal, 10 f., 16 ff., 28, 34, 37, 43, 56, 61, 64 f., 81, 86.
  apotropaic, 65.
  astral, 29 f., 34 f., 65, 86.
  biblical, 30, 34 ff., 57, 65 ff., 83 ff.
  floral and fruit, 10 f., 16 f., 20, 24 f., 28 f., 55, 67, 81, 83, 86.
  geometrical, 10, 16, 20, 22, 24, 28, 44, 67, 82, 86.
  human, 22, 24, 30, 34 ff., 61 ff., 83 ff.
  Jewish cycle, 30.
  Magic symbols, 16, 17[2], 65.
  mythological, 10, 24 f.
  ritual objects, 20, 30 f., 35, 37, 43, 53 ff., 67, 83, 86.

Na'aran, *v.* 'Ain Dûk.
Naḥûm, 7[1].
Names in inscriptions:
  Auxentios, 72; Baruch, 77; Benjamin, 73; Claudios Tiberios Polycharmos (Achyrios), 79 f.; Hanina, 77, 82; Herod, 71; Hezekia, 77;
  HLPW, 72; Hoples, 82; Ishmael, 60[1]; Johanan, 72; Jose, 71, 73, 77; Judan, 60[1], 77; Justos, 71, 75; Levi, 71; Marianos, 77; Moni(or, Moki-)mos, 71; Phineas, 75, 77; Photios, 82; Phroros, 82; Proton, 82; Sallustius, 82; Samuel, 77, 85; Simonides, 70; Theodoros, 44; Theodotos, 70; Vettenos, 70; Zebida, 72.
Niche as receptacle for Ark, 43, 83.
Nineveh, 3[1].
Noah, representation of Ark of, 36.

Offerings, 2.
Oliphant, Sir Lawrence, 4.
Ophel, synagogue at, 69.
Orfali, Père G., 5[1], 8, 20, 68[1], 71[4], 72[1].
Orientation, *v.* Synagogue.
Ornamentation, *v.* Motives, Synagogue.
Ossuaries, decoration of, 67.

Palestine Exploration Fund, excavations of, 4.
Palestine Government, Department of Antiquities, excavations of, 5, 22, 81, 85.
Palestine Historical and Ethnographical Society, Journal of the, 3.
Palestine, synagogues in, *v.* Place Names.
Palmyra, 68, 85.
Paul the Apostle, 49.
Peqi'in (Bukeia), synagogue at, 54.
Petrović, T., 79 f.
Philistines, representation of, 84 f.
Philo, 47, 66.
Pilgrims, Jewish, 2 f., 4, 71[1].
Pisces, *v.* Zodiac.
Plan of synagogues, *v.* Synagogue.
Plassart, A., 37[1], 38[2].
Portico, *v.* Synagogue.
Priene, synagogue at, 42 ff., 51.
Ptolemy III, 1[2].
Public worship, 47.

Râmeh, synagogue at, 25.
Rebellion, Jewish, in reign of Trajan, 48[1].
Reinach, T., 1[2], 70[1].
Renan, E., 2, 4, 68[1], 71[3].
Rheneia, 38[1].
Risom, Sven, 61[1].
Ritual objects, 20, 30 f., 35, 37, 43, 52 ff., 69, 83, 86.
Robinson, Edward, 3.
Rome, Catacombs at, 53, 56, 67.

Roof, *v.* Synagogue.
Ross, Ludwig, 44.
Rossi, de, 57.
Roussell, P., vii.

Sagittarius, *v.* Zodiac.
Sahl el-Baṭṭôff, 27.
Samuel, b. R. Samson, R., 3[1], 71.
Savignac, Père R., vii.
Schedia, 1[2].
Schrader, M., 42.
Schumacher, G., 4.
Schürer, 1[2], 38[2], 42.
Schwabe, M., vii, 80.
Screen, 57, 81.
Scroll of the Law, 18, 43, 52 f.
— cases, 53, 55[1].
Sculpture, 10 ff., 18 ff., 22 ff., 43, 55 f., 63 ff.
Seasons of the year, pictorial representation of, 30, 35, 86.
Seat of Moses, *v.* Moses.
Semmaka, synagogue at, 50, 85.
Sepphoris, 27.
Serbian Archaeological Society, excavations of, 79.
Sidon, 4.
Simeon ben Yohai, R., 3, 68.
Slouschz, N., 6[3], 55.
Sobernheim, M., 57.
Solomon, prayer of, 51 f.
— Temple of, 51, 57, 63.
— Throne of, 59.
Staircase, *v.* Synagogue.
Stobi, synagogue at, 79 f.
Strzygowski, 67.
Sun, Chariot of the, pictorial representation of, 29, 34, 86.
Synagogue:
accessories, 6, 35, 37, 52 ff., 67, 83, 86.
aisles, 13, 22, 24, 28, 46, 79, 86.
annexed chambers, 8, 12, 22, 28, 31, 38, 40, 48 f., 70, 79, 81.
apse, 27, 31, 35, 44, 52, 56 f., 79, 81.
architecture, 4 f., 8 ff., 21 ff., 24 ff., 40, 42 f., 68, 78 f., 81, 83, 86.
basilican types, 13, 22, 27 f., 31, 40, 42, 46, 48, 60[1], 79, 81, 86; (nonbasilican types, 38, 44, 83).
benches, 13, 32, 38, 40, 42, 47, 58, 81, 83.
building materials, 7 f., 12, 22, 57, 59 f.
ceiling tiles, 85.
class-room, 48.
colour, use of, in, 13, 29, 32, 44, 63, 66.

courtyard, 19 ff., 22, 28, 31, 40, 43, 79, 81, 83.
dating of, 27 f., 35, 40, 42, 45, 65, 68 f., 77, 79, 82, 85.
designation of, 37, 72 f., 76, 80.
entrance, 9 f., 12 f., 19, 27, 40, 44, 47, 83.
exploration of, 2 ff., 20 ff., 28, 31, 35, 37, 40, 42, 44 f., 61 f., 78, 79, 81 f., 85.
façade, 9 ff., 22, 24 f., 27.
floor, of flagstone, 21, 27; of mosaic, 6, 27 ff., 44, 56 f., 65, 72 ff., 81 f., 86.
frescoes, 65, 83 ff.
funds, 44, 80.
gallery, 8, 12, 14 ff., 22, 47 f.
gifts in honour of, 72.
hospice, 49, 70.
illumination, 11, 13, 74[1].
mural decoration, 16 ff., 22, 61 ff., 69, 83 ff.; and *v.* Motives, Sculpture.
orientation, 8, 18, 27, 43, 50 ff., 69, 79, 81, 83, 85 f.
origins, 1 f.
plans, 9, 23, 29, 32, 36, 39, 41, 43.
portico, 22, 24, 38, 40, 43, 48.
proprietorship, 74, 80.
roof, 15, 38, 81.
situation, 8, 37, 40, 42, 44, 49 f.
storeroom, 13.
windows, 11 ff., 22; arch of, 11, 22.

Titus, 17[1]; arch of, 63.
Tombs of Prophets, Saints, and Scholars, 2.

Ulai, river, 50.
Umm al-'Amad, synagogue at, 27.

Vincent, Father L. H., vii, 70[1], 73.

Warren, 4.
Water, in vicinity of synagogues, 49 f.
Watzinger, C., 5, 8, 17[2], 25, 27[1], 62[1], 68[1].
Weill, R., 69.
Welter, G., vii, 45.
Wiegand, Th., 42.
Wilson, C. W., 4, 7.
Women's Gallery, *v.* Synagogue.

Yale University, excavations of, 6, 82.
Yarmuk, river, 81.

Zodiac, signs of, 25, 26, 29, 34, 65, 66, 85, 86.

PLATES

PLATE I

a. Capernaum, north-west corner of synagogue, restored

b. Capernaum, northern colonnade of synagogue, restored

PLATE II

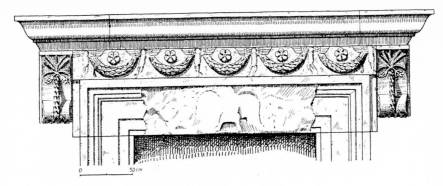

a. Capernaum, lintel of main doorway

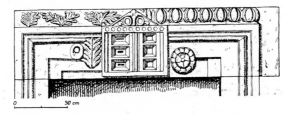

b. Capernaum, lintel of main gate to the courtyard

c. Capernaum, lintel of the second gate to the courtyard

PLATE III

a. Capernaum, keystone of arched window

b. Capernaum, frieze on the façade, defaced figure of lion

PLATE IV

a. Capernaum, benches on the west side

b. Capernaum, frieze

PLATE V

a. Capernaum, frieze

b. Capernaum, frieze

c. Capernaum, carruca

PLATE VI

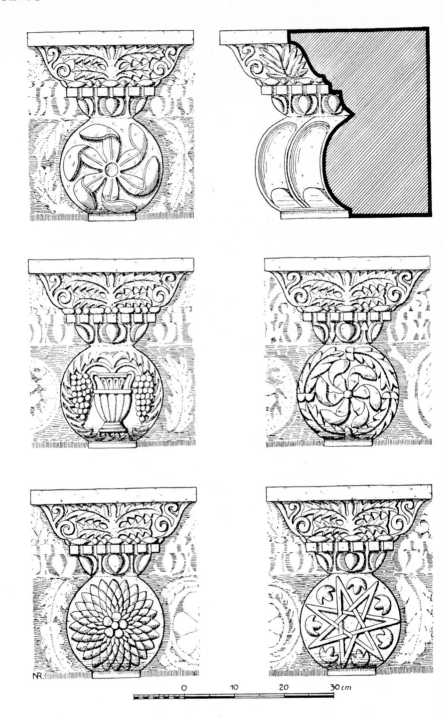

CAPERNAUM, STONES OF FRIEZE RESTING ON
PILASTER CAPITALS

PLATE VII

a. Capernaum, courtyard, corner capital

b. Capernaum, courtyard, capital

c. Capernaum, courtyard, capital

PLATE VIII

a. Chorazin, general view looking south

b. Chorazin, general view looking north-east

PLATE IX

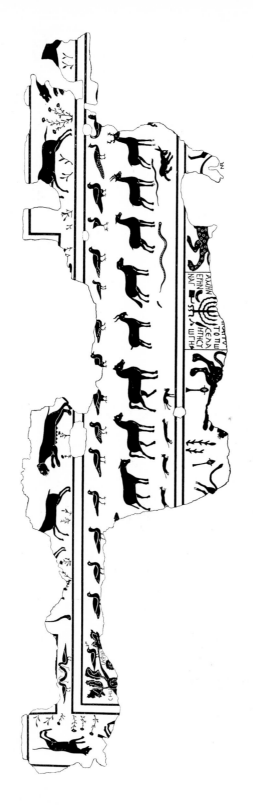

JERASH, SYNAGOGUE, MOSAIC FLOOR

PLATE X

DELOS, GENERAL VIEW OF SYNAGOGUE

PLATE XI

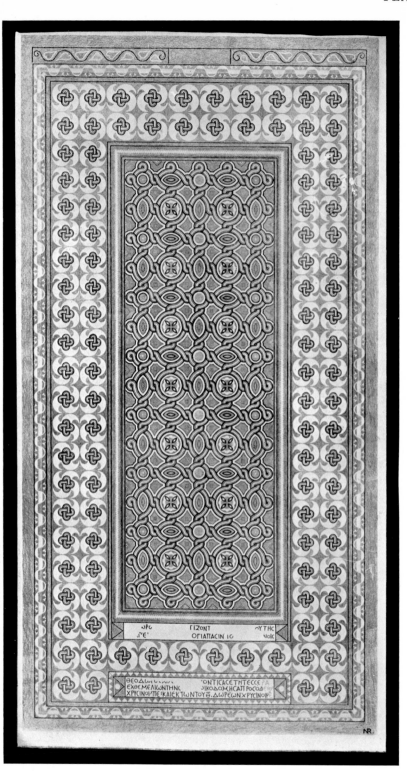

AEGINA, MOSAIC FLOOR OF SYNAGOGUE

PLATE XII

a. Ḥammath-by-Tiberias, stone candlestick

b. Ḥammath-by-Tiberias, screen

PLATE XIII

c. Kafr Bir'im, head of lion

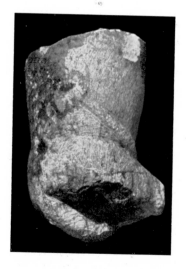

a

b

Capernaum, fragments of lion

PLATE XIV

ASCALON, SCREEN

PLATE XV

CHORAZIN, SEAT OF MOSES

PLATE XVI

a. Jerusalem, Ophel, inscription of Theodotos

b. Kafr Bir'im, doorway with inscribed lintel of small synagogue
(non-existent)

PLATE XVII

a. Capernaum, Greek inscription

b. Capernaum, Aramaic inscription

PLATE XVIII

a

b

NA'ARAN, MOSAIC INSCRIPTIONS

DATE DUE